Library of
Davidson College

SOVIET
MARXISM
AND
NUCLEAR WAR

Recent titles in
Contributions in Philosophy

Inquiries into Medieval Philosophy: A Collection in Honor of
Francis P. Clarke
James F. Ross, editor

The Vitality of Death: Essays in Existential Psychology and Philosophy
Peter Koestenbaum

Dialogues on the Philosophy of Marxism
Society for the Philosophical Study of Dialectical Materialism
John Somerville and Howard L. Parsons, editors

The Peace Revolution: Ethos and Social Process
John Somerville

Marx and Engels on Ecology
Howard L. Parsons, editor and compiler

The New Image of the Person: The Theory and Practice of Clinical Philosophy
Peter Koestenbaum

Panorama of Evil: Insights from the Behavioral Sciences
Leonard W. Doob

Alienation: From the Past to the Future
Ignace Feuerlicht

The Philosopher's World Model
Archie J. Bahm

Persons: A Comparative Account of the Six Possible Theories
F. F. Centore

Science, Animals, and Evolution: Reflections on Some Unrealized Potentials of Biology and Medicine
Catherine Roberts

The Philosophy of Human Rights: International Perspectives
Alan S. Rosenbaum, editor

Estrangement: Marx's Conception of Human Nature and the Division of Labor
Isidor Walliman

The Concept of Ideology and Political Analysis: A Critical Examination of Its Usage by Marx, Lenin, and Mannheim
Walter Carlsnaes

SOVIET MARXISM AND NUCLEAR WAR

AN INTERNATIONAL DEBATE

From the Proceedings of the Special Colloquium
of the XVth World Congress of Philosophy

Edited with an Introduction
by JOHN SOMERVILLE

Contributions in Philosophy, Number 18

GREENWOOD PRESS
WESTPORT, CONNECTICUT

Library of Congress Cataloging in Publication Data
Main entry under title:

Soviet Marxism and nuclear war.

(Contributions in philosophy ; no. 18 ISSN 0084-926X)
Includes index.
1. Communism and atomic warfare--Congresses.
I. Somerville, John, 1905-   II. World Congress of Philosophy.
HX545.S68   172'.42   80-25820
ISBN 0-313-22531-1 (lib. bdg.)

Copyright © 1981 by John Somerville

All rights reserved. No portion of this book may be reproduced, by any process or technique, without the express written consent of the publisher.

Library of Congress Catalog Card Number: 80-25820
ISBN: 0-313-22531-1
ISSN: 0084-926X

First published in 1981

Greenwood Press
A division of Congressional Information Service, Inc.
88 Post Road West, Westport, Connecticut 06881

Printed in the United States of America

10 9 8 7 6 5 4 3 2 1

Copyright Acknowledgment

The editor and publisher are grateful for permission to reprint from *Thirteen Days: A Memoir of the Cuban Missile Crisis*, by Robert F. Kennedy. Copyright © 1969 by W. W. Norton & Company, Inc. Reprinted by permission of W. W. Norton & Company, Inc., and Macmillan & Company Publishers.

Contents

    Introduction   vii

1. Soviet Marxism and Nuclear War
   JOHN SOMERVILLE (USA)   3

2. Technology, Peace, and Contemporary Marxism
   P. N. FEDOSEYEV (USSR)   17

3. Human Survival and Soviet Nuclear Policy
   SHINGO SHIBATA (JAPAN)   33

4. Nuclear Weapons, World Peace, and Contemporary Marxism
   DEBIPRASAD CHATTOPADHYAYA (INDIA)   55

5. Marxism-Leninism, World Peace, and World Revolution
   K. T. FANN (CANADA)   67

6. Why Socialism Needs Peace
   ERWIN HERLITZIUS (GDR)   75

7. Marxism, Technological Development, and World Peace
   ADAM SCHAFF (POLAND)   85

8. Are the Theses of Classical Marxism on Just War and Violence Valid Today?
   ADOLFO SÁNCHEZ VÁSQUEZ (MEXICO)   91

9. Psychology, Morality, and Nuclear Holocaust
   RONALD HIRSCHBEIN (USA)   97

10. Some Effects of Technology on the Prospects for Peace
    GEORGE H. HAMPSCH (USA)   109

11. Discussion and Replies 1
    V. V. SHELIAG (USSR)   121

    F. T. KONSTANTINOV (USSR)   125

    E. E. MODRZHINSKAIA (USSR)   127

    E. HERLITZIUS (GDR)   131

    K. T. FANN (CANADA)   135

    FRANZ LOESER (GDR)   139

12. Discussion and Replies 2
    RONALD HIRSCHBEIN (USA)   141

    HOWARD L. PARSONS (USA)   144

    JOHN SOMERVILLE (USA)   149

    Index   157

    About the Editor and Contributors   163

Introduction

The international debate among Marxists presented in this volume began at the XVth World Congress of Philosophy held in Varna, Bulgaria, in 1973, and was continued through subsequent correspondence, discussions, and research studies that carry the issues up to the present time. The countries represented in the discussion include the leading socialist and capitalist powers of the contemporary world.

This discussion taken as a whole marks the first and so far the only time that the problems involved in nuclear war have been publicly debated and explored in depth by Marxists who hold differing views on the subject. Thus, the present text constitutes a very significant contemporary document, one that throws strong light on what the whole world seems to agree is the most urgent problem of our time.

One must say *seems* to agree because this apparent agreement is strangely characterized by a certain abstractness, almost as if the concrete facts that constitute the problem were too frightening or too painful to confront directly. In a sense, this is the most dangerous aspect of our world situation because it really amounts to not confronting the problem at all. The virtue of this volume is that it does confront these facts directly and concretely. They form its point of departure and main focus. Let us emphasize them at the outset.

From the moment in 1945 when atomic fission was scientifically achieved and successfully applied to the production of a bomb, it was clear enough that the destructiveness of the nuclear weapon was so great, and continuous scientific progress in the increase of its destructiveness so certain, that the time would soon be reached when all-out war waged with such weapons could result in the annihilation of the human race.

That time has now arrived with a vengeance. Its general parameters were well described by U.S. Senator Patrick Leahy of Vermont during a remarkable Senate debate on foreign policy and nuclear war that took place in early June 1975. Leahy said: "We lose sight of the fact that we already have 615,835 times as much explosive power in nuclear weapons alone as the one bomb that was dropped on Hiroshima; that we have 8,000 nuclear warheads providing 36 nuclear weapons to target on each of the Soviet Union's 219 major urban areas, and we know damn well, Mr. President, that they have similar weapons targeted on us. We end up with enough weapons to kill every man, woman and child on this planet, and do it 27 times."[1] Since those words were spoken, whole new systems of nuclear weapons have been perfected on both sides, greatly increasing not only their number but also their accuracy and effectiveness, so that the index of overkill has risen proportionately, and continues to rise. At the present time (July 1981), it is conservatively estimated that U.S. arsenals contain between 25,000 and 30,000 nuclear weapons while production continues at the rate of about five new weapons every twenty-four hours, as if there were an irresistible compulsion to be able to go on killing those already dead.

There are understandable reasons why people want to "lose sight" of such facts: they are very unpleasant to think about, and their implications (the irreversible ending of the human world along with the total extermination of all forms of life on the planet Earth) are so vast and staggering that they are extremely hard to believe, as distinguished from understand. The very magnitude of these enormities is so great as to pressure the mind into wishful thinking that quickly embraces such conclusions as that these very facts mean that such things will never come about, that human beings would never make the decisions that they know would have such results; or that if people are capable of making such decisions, then we can do nothing about it, so there is no use in thinking or talking about the matter.

It is scarcely necessary to point out that these reasons why people "lose sight" of such facts are transparently childish and quite inconsistent with what everyone knows and does every day. If such reasons were valid, they would mean that we should not try to give constructive thought and action to the prevention of such things as genocide or gang rape, or the promotion of drug addiction among children, since their consequences are so horrible that human beings would never decide to bring these things about, and if they were capable of so deciding, then there is nothing we can do about it. Such thinking is grounded in the absurd premise, born of panic, that the more monstrous the possible consequences, the less reason there is for us to give thought and action to preventing them.

In any case, the last escape hatch to these illusory comforts of wishful thinking about nuclear war was slammed shut forever by the Kennedy administration during the Cuban missile crisis of 1962. This "murder of a beautiful theory by a gang of brutal facts" took the form of a deliberate, wholly conscious decision made by the president and supported by a special group of top advisers who acknowledged its world-ending implications with complete candor. (Equally significant is the fact that it was also supported by the heads of the British, French, and West German governments.) The decision was to send an ultimatum to the Soviet government to remove its missile bases from Cuba unilaterally (that is, without the United States removing its own similar bases from Turkey) within twenty-four hours or the United States would destroy the Soviet missiles in Cuba by invasion and bombing. The American leaders, by their own admission, *did not expect* the Soviets to obey the ultimatum and *did expect* the resulting war to be nuclear and to bring about "the end of mankind." These are Robert Kennedy's own words in his posthumously published memoir, *Thirteen Days*, detailing the crisis in which he played a central part. (The full documentation is given and discussed in chapter 1 of the present volume.) The only reason mankind did not come to an end on that occasion was that the Soviets *unexpectedly* decided to obey the ultimatum.

Unhappily, since actions speak louder than words, there is every indication that the lesson drawn from the Cuban missile crisis by all the administrations after Kennedy's is that nuclear weaponry, along with the tactic of openly threatening nuclear war, is the best basis for American foreign policy, especially for meeting the competitive challenge that socialism and communism present to capitalism. How else could one explain the fact that President Nixon, the inheritor of Johnson's undeclared war in Vietnam, boldly blockaded Haiphong harbor, as Kennedy had blockaded Cuba, and publicly threatened our fellow nuclear superpower, the Soviet Union, with the destruction of its ships if it tried to send anything to Hanoi, exactly as Kennedy had threatened the Soviet Union in the case of Cuba? How else could one explain the fact that President Ford did not repudiate the public policy statement of his secretary of defense, James Schlesinger, who said, "Under no circumstances could we disavow the first use of nuclear weapons," adding that the most likely target of such first use would be "Soviet military installations"?[2]

How else could one explain the fact that President Carter appointed the same James Schlesinger to his Cabinet and, in his first policy speech before the United Nations, on October 4, 1977, declared that he would be first to use nuclear weapons in case of anything he deemed an "attack," whether "nuclear *or conventional*," (italics added) against not only our own country, but any of our "allies," numbering no fewer than sixty by treaty, or against any of our "armed forces" scattered on more than 400 bases around the globe? How else could one explain the fact that President Carter did not accept the offer made by the Soviet Union in 1976, repeated in 1979 and 1980, to sign a mutual declaration that neither side would be the first to use nuclear weapons? How else could one explain the fact that President Reagan also refuses these offers?

To these central political facts must be added certain central technological facts emphasized by Robert C. Aldridge, who, "during sixteen years in the engineering department of Lockheed, the nation's number one arms producer, helped design every submarine-launched ballistic missile the Navy has bought."[3] In a speech in Tokyo in August 1978, he said:

> I feel we are in the middle, right now, of another major escalation in the arms race. We are departing from what used to be the deterrent strategy and have moved towards a counterforce strategy, which is rapidly moving towards a first-strike strategy. I think the time is more critical than at any other escalation in the arms race so far. I feel we have, at the most, four or five years to change the direction that the world is going, especially in my country, the United States. I feel that nuclear weapons will be used, and I think history bears this out, in a first-strike strategy. When nuclear weapons or any weapon or weapons system has been developed it is always used. . . . About two years ago, I started devoting full-time to research in submarine warfare. The things I found were really frightening to me. Then I started looking at other aspects of the first strike: space warfare, ballistic missile defense, etc., and found that all technologies under development were to launch a pre-emptive first strike.[4]

These are some of the concrete facts that make up the situation that confronts contemporary Marxism and Communist governments in relation to nuclear war. To put it bluntly, they are confronted with nuclear blackmail that now deliberately rejects *mutual* deterrence in favor of unilateral threat of first use. It could not honestly be said that this is the situation that equally confronts contemporary capitalism and the U.S. government. For it is obvious that the nuclear blackmail is not mutual since this blackmail is precisely the threat of first use and this threat is made by only one side, which at the same time rejects the offer of the other side to sign a mutual disavowal of first use. Nor could it be said that the U.S. government is confronted by any government that ever made a deliberate decision that it consciously expected to result in the end of humankind.

Neither could it be said that capitalism is confronted by a competing economic system that welcomes, and to a significant extent depends on, the profits that can be made out of producing the weapons of war. The possible cessation of war production, of "defense contracts," is widely considered by capitalist leaders to be as serious a threat to the stability of the capitalist economy as the same possibility is considered by communist leaders to be a welcome prospect that would greatly help to fulfill the plans of the socialist economy. The conclusion is inescapable that one system is willing to disavow nuclear weapons and compete peacefully on a basis of reciprocity, while the other system is not. In effect, one side has proposed peaceful coexistence, and the other has replied, better dead than red.

But all this gives no easy answer to the question of what contemporary Marxism in general, or the Soviet Union in particular, should do in relation to the possibility of nuclear war. Of course, everyone agrees that everyone should try to prevent it. But what if, in spite of all preventive efforts, a "crisis" arises somewhere —in Korea, the Middle East, Africa, or anywhere else—and the U.S. government sends another ultimatum, in the style of the Cuban missile crisis? Or what if an actual nuclear attack is made, perhaps against "Soviet military installations"? What should Marxist governments then do? Should all-out nuclear war—and the end of mankind—then be accepted? This is what is so difficult, and the reader of this volume will see how differently different Marxists answer such a question.

In any case, it is obvious that the consequences of nuclear war are so threatening to everything human that everything human that wants to survive must take thought and action, must take stock of all its creative resource as never before, and must apply them to this problem, on the solution of which everything else now depends.

NOTES

1. *Congressional Record*, June 2, 1975, p. S9233.
2. Quoted in *The New York Times*, July 2, 1975.
3. Robert C. Aldridge, *The Counterforce Syndrome: A Guide to U.S. Nuclear Weapons and Strategic Doctrine* (Washington, D.C.: Institute for Policy Studies, 1978).
4. See *Documents of 1978 World Conference for Nuclear Disarmament, Tokyo, Hiroshima, Nagasaki, August 1-9, 1978*, pp. 26-27.

SOVIET MARXISM AND NUCLEAR WAR

1
Soviet Marxism and Nuclear War
JOHN SOMERVILLE (USA)

In this paper, I shall try to answer three questions. First, what was the position of classical Marxism on the use and justification of war? Second, what is the significance of the changes that the technological revolution has brought about in the weaponry of war since the days of Marx and Engels? Third, what conclusions follow if to the contemporary problem of the use and justification of war we apply the historical thesis central to Marx's whole view of society—that qualitative changes made by human beings at the technological base of society demand corresponding changes at superstructural levels such as moral and political principles?

The position of classical Marxism on the use and justification of war is generally well known.[1] Emphasis was given to the fact that capitalism breeds wars, that throughout its history the economics of private property has led to the politics of war, that the predatory seizure of raw materials and markets abroad has been the natural accompaniment of class exploitation at home. Morally, the Marxist position in general, and the Soviet position in particular, has been that war in itself is not a good thing since it involves the killing and injuring of human beings as well as the destruction of material goods, but that it is justified when it represents an act of collective self-defense. That is, when force and violence are used against people in violation of their human rights, such people have the right to use force and violence in return in order to defend themselves and preserve their rights. This is the moral basis of the concept of the just war. In other words, there is such a thing as a just war only because there is such a thing as social and international injustice. When there is a society of human justice and abundance on a worldwide scale, as Marx and Engels conceived of fully developed communism, the need for war will disappear, and the state apparatus of physical violence—armies, navies, air forces, and police forces—will be able to "wither away," as Engels put it.[2] But until this condition is reached, the use of war remains politically and morally acceptable if its use represents an act of collective self-defense made necessary by the violence of aggressors.

It is not difficult to see that a central and necessary part of this position of classical Marxism concerning the justification of war was the implicit assumption that the war would not be fought with weapons of total destructiveness, weapons capable, in their technological development, of eliminating all forms of life from the planet Earth. There is no evidence that it ever occurred to Marx or Engels that, by the middle of the twentieth century, such weapons would already have been produced. But suppose such a possibility had occurred to someone who then asked Marx or Engels: "Could a just war be fought with such weapons?" Is it likely that Marx or Engels would have replied: "One always has the right of self-defense; if one is attacked with thermonuclear weapons, one has the right to fight back with thermonuclear weapons, even though in the end the human race would be destroyed"? It seems to me more likely that Marx and Engels would have replied along these lines: "When we speak of a just war, we mean that one of the sides is by armed force defending its lives, rights, and material goods because the other side used armed force that threatened to destroy those lives, rights, and material goods. But if the kind of armed force used by both sides leads, in its overall result, to the destruction of the human race, then it is not a just war on either side. Even from the point of view of those originally attacked and wronged, such a war is a remedy worse than the disease, like killing oneself to overcome an attack of pneumonia. Such a war is not self-defense, but self-destruction, and not only self-destruction, but omni-destruction. It would be stupid and immoral in the highest possible degree."

This reply is only common sense. To make it, Marx would not need to be Marx, so to speak; he would only need to be a person of average or normal intelligence. By the same token, it might seem that the solution of the problem is equally obvious to common sense. That is, it might seem that the solution is simply to eliminate those particular weapons and go back to fighting wars, when wars are necessary, with the old weapons, which are less than totally destructive, so that there will always be a habitable planet and a human race left when the war is over. Put in legal and diplomatic terms, this solution would be that all states that possess nuclear weapons should come to an agreement that such weapons must not be used, that they must be destroyed, and that no more of them are to be produced. How should we evaluate this idea?

Although an agreement of this kind would be a good thing, everyone will understand upon reflection that it could not by itself be relied on as a genuine solution of the problem. For it is impossible to destroy the scientific knowledge of how to produce the totally destructive weapons, and if a fight to the finish should break out among the major powers, each side could be expected to assume that the other side would try not only to resume production of the old totally destructive weapons but also to produce new varieties of like destructiveness. So each side would again be moved to arm itself with such weapons. Even in peacetime, it is impossible to prevent scientific research from discovering, even without intending to do so, further and further possibilities of such weaponry. And all experience shows that when nations feel their existence is at stake, or governments are seized with ambitions for conquest, treaties are readily broken.

Moreover, there is no sign that the historical dynamic of the revolution in science and technology is slowing down or coming to an end. On the contrary, we can only assume that all the scientific and technological progress made so far is but a beginning and that this progress will continue accelerating—to outcomes at present quite unimaginable. There is no way to prevent this ongoing technological progress from including actual or potential applications to the field of weaponry, for weapons themselves are nothing but machines, technical devices, and scientifically controlled physical and chemical processes applied to destructive uses. This means we can formulate a historical law: technological progress in the means of production implies the possibility of like progress in the means of destruction. This law reflects a very important part of the history of science and technology.

One result of the operation of this historical law has been that from this point on we must all live with the knowledge that, in spite of any agreements signed by the major powers, if, subsequently, war should break out among them, the probability that such a war would result in the annihilation of the human race increases significantly with each passing year. What can we do about a situation of this kind? On the surface, it might seem that the answer has already been given by classical Marxism, in the form of the teaching about war that we referred to at the outset. That is, in the modern world, the principal cause of wars is capitalism. When capitalism as an economic system is replaced with socialism-communism on a world scale, then the danger of large-scale war will disappear.

But of course, classical Marxism equally emphasizes that the process of replacing capitalism with socialism-communism is one that will be resisted by capitalism with all the weapons at its disposal, including especially the most highly developed weapons of physical destructiveness. To Marx and Engels, this meant that the forces of socialism-communism must be prepared to fight back with the same weapons, even more highly developed if possible, in the decisive struggles against capitalism. Today, this would mean that the forces of socialism-communist must be prepared to fight back with bigger and "better" thermonuclear weapons and others of similar destructive power. Since it is now likely that such a contest would destroy the human race, it is impossible to believe that Marx and Engels would now take the same view that they did in their time. Therefore, they would have to look further for a solution of this historically unprecedented problem, as we today must do.

What alternatives have been presented in our time? Actually, there has been relatively little Marxist discussion of this problem —the specific problem of fighting wars with weapons that can end the human world—in spite of the tremendous import of the problem. However, when it is discussed among Marxists, perhaps the most frequent line of thought presented is as follows: the very fact that these weapons are possessed by the forces of socialism-communism will prevent the other side from using its own weapons of this kind because it too knows that a contest fought out with them would destroy the human race. Thus, the suggestion is that the problem, in a sense, is its own solution. That is, the very existence of such weapons on both sides is a guarantee that neither side would deliberately make a decision that would bring them into play since neither side would deliberately choose to end the human world.

Unfortunately, this comforting theory was completely disproved by the actual facts of the Cuban missile crisis of 1962— the facts that were revealed only in 1968 in Robert Kennedy's posthumously published account of the American government's decision-making process during the crisis. Let us examine these facts rather closely, as they measure the gravity of the problem better than anything else. At that time, Robert Kennedy's brother, John Kennedy, was president of the United States, and Robert, who was attorney general, was a leading member of the group of top officials who assisted President Kennedy in making the final decisions in the crisis. Robert Kennedy's detailed and candid revelations of the thought processes and weighing of values that entered into the American government's decisions unquestionably make his little book one of the most important documents published in the twentieth century. Relative to the specific possibility of the human race being destroyed by deliberate decision, it must be called the most important document ever published. The book bears the title, *Thirteen Days: A Memoir of the Cuban Missile Crisis*.[3] The original edition, which appeared in

McCall's magazine, carried the subtitle, *The Story About How the World Almost Ended*.[4]

Incredible as it may seem, this subtitle is entirely warranted by the facts set forth in the document. The chief facts are as follows:

    1. It was acknowledged by President Kennedy and his advisers that the Soviet Union had the same legal right to accept Cuba's invitation to set up missile bases in Cuba as the United States had to accept Turkey's invitation to set up missile bases in Turkey,[5] which is, of course, closer to the Soviet Union than Cuba is to the United States.

    2. However, the setting up of the missile bases in Cuba evidently took the American government by surprise, and the bases were looked upon as an intolerable threat. President Kennedy ordered an armed blockade of Cuba and announced to the world that any attempt to deliver additional missiles to Cuba would be prevented by force.[6]

    3. Soviet Chairman Khrushchev proposed that the matter be settled peacefully by the simultaneous removal of the Soviet missiles from Cuba and the American missiles from Turkey.[7]

    4. President Kennedy and his advisers rejected this offer and decided to send the Soviet government an ultimatum to the effect that, if the Soviet side did not undertake to remove its missiles unilaterally and immediately, they would be bombed and destroyed by American forces. American planes equipped with nuclear bombs were placed in the air on continuous patrol.[8]

    5. President Kennedy acknowledged that he did not expect the Soviet government to obey the ultimatum and did expect that he would have to order the bombing of the Soviet missile bases. He further expected that the Soviets would then fight back, and that the war between the United States and the Soviet Union would become a global thermonuclear holocaust that would destroy the human race and end the human world. These expectations were shared by his advisers. They faced all these consequences of the decision to send the ultimatum,

but nevertheless, a majority agreed with the decision to send it.[9]

The citations to these five points indicate the confirming passages in Robert Kennedy's text. Actually, the first four are matters of historical record and may be found in many sources. That which is unique to Robert Kennedy's book, and which represents the heart of this unprecedented, incredible situation, is expressed in point five. Let us therefore quote in full Robert Kennedy's own words, beginning with his account of the conversation he had with Soviet Ambassador Dobrynin, on the instructions of President Kennedy, in order to convey to the Soviets the seriousness of the decision that the American government had made.

He told Dobrynin that:

> we had to have a commitment by tomorrow that those bases would be removed.... He should understand that if they did not remove those bases, we would remove them.... Perhaps his country might feel it necessary to take retaliatory action; but before that was over, there would be not only dead Americans but dead Russians as well. He asked me what offer the United States was making, and I told him of the letter that President Kennedy had just transmitted to Khrushchev. He raised the question of our removing the missiles from Turkey. I said there could be no quid pro quo or any arrangement made under this kind of threat or pressure.... We had only a few more hours—we needed an answer immediately from the Soviet Union. I said we must have it the next day. I returned to the White House. The President was not optimistic, nor was I. He ordered twenty-four troop carrier squadrons of the Air Force Reserve to active duty. They would be necessary for an invasion. He had not abandoned hope, but what hope there was now rested with Khrushchev's revising his course within the next few hours. It was a hope, not an expectation. The expectation was a military confrontation by Tuesday and possibly tomorrow.[10]

Thus, the actual expectation, as distinguished from the forlorn hope, was that the Soviets would not unilaterally remove their missile bases and that American forces would have to destroy them by an armed invasion, which would be the beginning of open war between the United States and the Soviet Union. The expectation of the scope and nature of the war is likewise carefully delineated by Robert Kennedy. Throughout his account, he makes it clear that they all realized that what they were deciding about was a world war and a nuclear war that would annihilate humankind. In this connection, Kennedy writes: "These hourly decisions, necessarily made with such rapidity, could be made only by the President of the United States, but any one of them might close and lock doors for peoples and governments in many other lands. We had to be aware of this responsibility at all times, he [the President] said, aware that we were deciding, the President was deciding, for the U.S., the Soviet Union, Turkey, Nato, and really for all mankind. . . ."[11] Again referring to the president, and the character of the war that was expected by him and the others, Robert Kennedy writes: "The thought that disturbed him the most, and that made the prospect of war much more fearful than it would otherwise have been, was the specter of the death of the children of this country and all the world—the young people who had no role, who had no say, who knew nothing even of the confrontation, but whose lives would be snuffed out like everyone else's."[12] Robert Kennedy expresses the same thought on his own account in the very first page of his memoir: "This was the beginning of the Cuban missile crisis—a confrontation between the two giant atomic nations, the U.S. and the U.S.S.R., which brought the world to the abyss of nuclear destruction and the end of mankind."

Even though these were the consequences that the president and his advisers *expected* to follow from the decision to order the Soviets to remove their missile bases from Cuba unilaterally, or have them bombed, the president and his advisers felt that the ultimatum must be delivered, and it was in fact delivered. In other words, the total destruction of the human race was deliberately chosen in preference to a simultaneous removal of the Soviet missiles from Cuba and the American missiles from Turkey. To compound the incredible, it was agreed by the president and his advisers that our Turkish missiles actually were "clearly obsolete," but nevertheless should not be withdrawn under any "threat from the Soviet Union."[13]

At the end of Robert Kennedy's posthumously published memoir, a pathetic note is appended by his friend and presumptive editor, Theodore Sorensen, who, as presidential counsel, was himself a member of the group of advisers. The note reads as follows: "It was Senator Kennedy's intention to add a discussion of the basic ethical question involved: what, if any, circumstance or justification gives this government or any government the moral right to bring its people and possibly all people under the shadow of nuclear destruction? He wrote this book in the summer and fall of 1967 on the basis of his personal diaries, and recollections, but never had an opportunity to re-write or complete it."[14] It is not surprising that Robert Kennedy was conscious of the problem of trying to find a moral justification for the kind of decision that was made, a justification that would look convincing when put on paper; it is even less surprising that he did not find any. For what could possibly justify the total destruction of the human race, which means not only the total destruction of all presently existing human life and human values but also the destruction of the entire human future with all its infinite human potentialities—a crime so unspeakable that it does not even have a name?

And yet the deliberate decision that was consciously expected to have precisely this result was taken by highly educated individuals who were in many other respects morally sensitive. How could that be possible? I have examined elsewhere the psychological and sociocultural conditions that could account for the empirical fact of such a decision on the part of such individuals and also for the fact, equally incredible morally, that it caused no outcry of indignation from the general public.[15] But what concerns us here, and creates our most urgent contemporary problem, is the evident fact itself, which can be stated in this way: the conscious expectation on the part of educated statesmen that certain actions, if taken, will bring about the total destruction of the human race cannot by itself be counted on to deter them from taking these actions.

Does classical or contemporary Marxism offers us anything effective on which we might build in trying to solve this problem, which has now become, in the most literal sense, the precondition to the solution of all other social problems? If Marxism offers us something to build upon (and I think it does), it is not the idea that capitalism will first be defeated in some final, all-out war, after which there will be a firm basis for world peace. As we can see today, after such a war there would indeed be peace, but there would no longer be a human race. Neither is it the idea that the possession, by both sides, of weapons capable of annihilating the human race is a guarantee that such weapons would not be used by either side. As we see from the Cuban missile crisis, there is no such guarantee. One side expected to use them.

Marxism offers us something else. It is not a solution already perfected, but a basis from which we can hope to reach a perfected solution. It is implicit in the profound, many-sided thought we referred to at the outset: that the fundamental dynamic of human history can be traced to the changes made by human beings at the technological base of their society, that is, in the tools, forces, materials, and methods of human production. The changes made at this basic level become the principal determinants of changes at the superstructual level, which includes politics and morality. As Marx put it at the beginning of his *Contribution to the Critique of Political Economy*: "The mode of production in material life determines the general character of the social, political and spiritual processes of life."[16] In other words, when human beings make qualitative changes in the powers and methods of production, they create new demands, possibilities, needs, and conditions that can find their outlet, implementation, and satisfaction only through corresponding qualitative changes in politics, morality, law, education, and other social institutions and agencies. Humankind has so far survived and progressed because it has been able to make such changes, and to make them in time—not as automatic responses, but by the exercise of creative initiative arising out of intelligence, courage, and moral feeling.

Today, it is quite clear that the technological means of production have undergone qualitative changes, manifested most dramatically in the new power given by atomic fission and fusion. Applied constructively, this gigantic new power might (or at least in the beginning we thought it might) be the energy basis for a new life on Earth for humankind. Applied destructively, it can certainly terminate all life on Earth. Human beings, therefore, need a new theory and practice of morals and politics to go with this new power, in order to continue to survive and progress. The old theory and practice of the morals and politics of war reflect an older, qualitatively different situation.

This means that we must reexamine all the inherited habits, attitudes, principles, and practices connected with the morality and politics of war, in light of the consequences of the new weapons with which wars can now be fought. This calls for new researches of all kinds in terms of educational methods and political strategies as they relate to the practice and nonpractice of war under the present conditions. All this is difficult, to say the least. It is bound to disturb present patterns of operation and can easily become an object of suspicion on the part of established authority, wherever that authority lacks revolutionary creativity.

It is extremely significant that a beginning has nonetheless been made by contemporary Marxism, an example of which can be seen in the very matter we have been discussing—the Cuban missile crisis. All the old habits, practices, and principles would have led the Soviet government to refuse to remove its missiles from Cuba unless the Americans agreed to remove theirs from Turkey simultaneously, that it should prefer to resist the Americans with armed force and return bomb for bomb rather than submit to the deprivation of equal rights. At the time, not a few people criticized the Soviet government for removing its missiles unilaterally, on the ground that the major Communist power would then become discredited in the eyes of the world, would lose political influence, and would henceforth be unable to do anything in international affairs that would seriously challenge the interests of the American government. Actually, the opposite result came about. Throughout most of the world, the

Soviet government gained moral respect and political credit for preventing the Cuban missile crisis from exploding into the thermonuclear holocaust of World War III, and the Soviet Union shortly thereafter established a major presence in the Middle East, significantly changing the balance of power there. In any case, the Soviet government acted on the principle that it is better to accept a temporary defeat (better to give in, when necessary, to nuclear blackmail) than to enter into a war that would destroy the human world, that is, a war fought with nuclear weapons on both sides.

This is, of course, but one example, the theoretical implications of which have not been explicitly worked out in relation to the problem as a whole, which remains to challenge us. We must meet that challenge in its fullest sense. There is no other path to the human future.

NOTES

1. An exception is the question of the Marxist preconditions for entering into a revolutionary civil war for the overthrow of an existing government. In bourgeois countries in general and in the United States in particular, the false opinion that these preconditions do not include the necessity of having majority support for forcible action against the government in question is not only widespread but is, one may say, intensively cultivated. This distortion (that Marxists believe in minority coups), a weapon used by reactionaries indiscriminately against radicals, is often made a part of law by being explicitly incorporated into legislative enactments as the justification for measures depriving communists of rights and privileges enjoyed by others. See John Somerville, *The Communist Trials and the American Tradition: Expert Testimony on Force and Violence* (New York: Cameron, 1956); "Law, Logic and Revolution: The Smith Act Decisions," *Western Political Quarterly* (December 1961); "Problems of Legal Reasoning in the US Since World War II Concerning Forcible Revolution," *Logique et Analyse*, No. 53-54, from *Proceedings of World Congress for Legal and Political Philosophy* (Brussels: 1971).

2. Friedrich Engels, *Anti-Dühring* (New York: International, n.d.), pp. 314-15.

3. Robert F. Kennedy, *Thirteen Days: A Memoir of the Cuban Missile Crisis* (New York: W. W. Norton, New American Library, 1969).

4. *McCall's* magazine, November 1968.
5. Kennedy, *Thirteen Days*, pp. 94, 95.
6. Ibid., pp. 55, 135, 140-43.
7. Ibid., p. 94.
8. Ibid., p. 108.
9. Ibid., pp. 98-99, 106.
10. Ibid., p. 108.
11. Ibid., p. 99. Kennedy does not explain by what moral calculus decisions that were acknowledged to involve the final destruction of the entire human race had to be made with such rapidity. What is even stranger, coming from the attorney general of the United States, is the view that the decision to initiate war can be made "only by the President." The Constitution of the United States clearly and explicitly states that such a decision is to be made only by the Congress (Art. I, Sect. 8, 11). The president, as commander-in-chief, may order immediate reply by force to any sudden attack, but the decision that such a reply is to be followed up by large-scale, sustained war, and the decision to initiate acts of war in the absence of a direct attack, that is, to make war as a matter of policy (which was the issue in the Cuban missile crisis), are deliberately withheld from the president and given to Congress. Abraham Lincoln (in a letter to Herndon) emphasized that "The provision of the Constitution giving the war-making power to Congress" came from the fact that the American Founding Fathers understood this power "to be the most oppressive of all kingly oppressions, and they resolved to so frame the Constitution that no one man should hold the power . . . "—quoted in Francis Wormuth, *The Vietnam War: The President Versus the Constitution* (Santa Barbara, Calif.: Center for the Study of Democratic Institutions, 1968), p. 11. Presidents initiate war when they have reason to believe Congress would not do so. For data relative to the Vietnam war in this regard, see John Somerville, "The Relation of Morality and Law to Contemporary Youth Protests in the United States" (VIIth World Congress of Sociology, Varna, 1971). For further analysis of the problem of American presidential war and world peace, see idem, *Durchbruch zum Frieden: Eine amerikanische Gesellschaftskritik* (Darmstadt: Verlag Darmstädter Blätter, 1973), chapters 1 and 2, translated by Günther Schwarz. The original English title of this work was *The Peace Revolution: Ethos and Social Process*. Subsequently, it appeared in Japanese translation by Shingo Shibata (Tokyo: Iwanami Shoten Publishers, 1974), and was published in English in 1975 by Greenwood Press, Westport, Connecticut, and London, England.

12. Kennedy, *Thirteen Days*, p. 106.
13. Ibid., pp. 94-95.
14. Ibid., p. 108.
15. Somerville, *The Peace Revolution*, especially chapter 5.
16. Karl Marx, *Contribution to the Critique of Political Economy* (Chicago: Kerr, 1904), p. 12. Also in John Somerville and Ronald E. Santoni, *Social and Political Philosophy: Readings from Plato to Gandhi* (New York: Doubleday, 1963), p. 379.

2
Technology, Peace, and Contemporary Marxism
P. N. FEDOSEYEV (USSR)

In my report, I would like to touch on a few philosophical questions related to the topic under discussion. First, I would like to say that I agree with what Academician Todor Pavlov had to say about the assessment and consequences of a possible thermonuclear war. He was quite right in saying that we should not intimidate ourselves and, with a feeling of doom, say that life on our planet is going to be destroyed in the event of a nuclear war and that the "end of the world" will come. At the same time, he rightly stressed that we should not underestimate the danger of such a war nor take the possible consequences lightly. With technological development at its present level, a world thermonuclear war carries with it the danger of a terrible catastrophe, and everyone should understand this. That is why we disagree with the view voiced by one speaker that a nuclear war might bring a bright future nearer.

There is no nation on Earth for which a world war would be in its vital interest and would be dictated by the needs of its progressive development. No sensible person would ever think that a world war might be progressive and just. The only kind of people who could think in terms of a world war are the madmen who want to "have done with communism," to destroy the socialist countries. They are afraid of communism more than they are afraid of mankind's destruction. Their motto is "Better dead than red."

Of course, there are people of an adventurist cast of mind who say that it is worth risking a world war for the sake of creating a better society, and that the destruction and casualties will be justified by the happiness of future generations. We cannot consider people Marxists who say that in the third world war the world proletariat and the revolutionary peoples would lose only their chains and would receive in return "a bright red new world." Only chauvinists who have completely broken with Marxism in practice and in theory can think like that. Communists cannot assume the responsibility for such adventurist slogans. Marxist-Leninists vigorously expose such views as dangerous to humanity.

Whoever wants to play with fire, to lay the lives of peoples at stake, whoever is ready to sacrifice hundreds of millions of people in a war of destruction, does not stand on Marxist positions, but on positions of political adventurism, and does great harm to the world liberation movement.

Communists treat the problems of war and peace with all seriousness. They cannot live just for today, not caring what happens to the world after they are gone. Their policy is based on their readiness to answer to history for the fate of peoples, for the present and future of mankind. Lenin considered it a crime to draw nations into war.

The main thing, of course, is not merely to argue about what percent of the lives and material values on Earth will be destroyed as a consequence of a possible thermonuclear war. The main thing is to undertake every measure to prevent it. The most effective measure in this respect would be to ban forever and destroy all nuclear weapons and biological and chemical means of mass destruction. The interests of peace call for arms reduction and the implementation of such a radical measure as universal and complete disarmament. And we can note with satisfaction that the progressive public and many statesmen in the world understand this task and that a constant campaign is being conducted for its accomplishment. The Soviet Union is consistently implementing the Peace Program set forth by the XXIVth Congress of the CPSU, a program for the vigorous defense of peace and the strengthening of international security.

Much has been said in this debate about the Cuban missile

crisis. Quotations from Robert Kennedy's memoirs and from other sources have been cited. I would like to say that in many American works, including those memoirs, the idea is put forward that that crisis reflected the competition between the nuclear powers and was at the same time a contest of wills, a struggle of determination, a psychological conflict. To be sure, political blackmail was used in this case to no small extent, since the leaders of the United States at that time loudly proclaimed their readiness to give the signal to use atomic bombs.

Without going into the details of the memoirs of different political figures, I would like to say that in my view the essence of the matter consisted of something else entirely. The whole point was that the Soviet Union and the socialist countries had as their objective to help socialist Cuba protect its independence. This had to be done in such a way as to avoid a thermonuclear war and to preserve peace. This was precisely the crux of the situation at that time, and this was precisely what the essence of our policy was. More than ten years have passed since then, and the fact remains that Cuba still exists, that it has preserved and strengthened its independence, and that it is developing successfully. Here we see that the prediction about the possibility of helping Cuba defend its independence was translated into reality. Ten years after that crisis, we continue to live without a nuclear war, and I am happy to say that the chances of preventing such a war are now (1973) even better than before.

Now about just and unjust wars. We have been discussing this question with John Somerville over a long period, and we continued our debate during the meetings of the American Philosophical Association in the spring of 1969 in Cleveland.

Apparently, Somerville proceeds from the view that since a nuclear world war would now lead to the annihilation of mankind and of all life on Earth, the question of just wars is thereby eliminated. Whatever goals a war might pursue, be they the most noble and idealistic, with such an outcome, that is, with the destruction of the greater part of all mankind, it could not be considered just nor be justified by anything. Thus, speaking in Cleveland on the problems of war and peace, Somerville stated the question in the following way: If in contemporary conditions a given war could lead to the destruction of the whole human race and all life on Earth, could such a war be called really just? He replied to this question in the negative. Naturally, Somerville is aware that, from the point of view of the traditional criteria of a just war, there are, as he puts it, clear cases, such as, for example, a war for national liberation. But the prospect of a nuclear war compels him and others who think like him to reconsider the traditional criteria and to deny that a just war is possible in the nuclear age.

Of course, in these arguments, there is a definite problem connected with the change in the nature of weapons and the probable consequences of a world war in the present epoch. Somerville, I think, feels that if we acknowledge the just nature of a thermonuclear war as applied to some particular country, this would be detrimental to the cause of defending peace and the struggle against the danger of war.

The question of the class criteria of war, however, is not eliminated. The fact that, because of the existence of massive means of destruction, war as a means of policy carries a threat to human civilization does not at all mean that, from the standpoint of its class content, war has ceased to be the continuation of a definite policy by other, nonpeaceful means. That is precisely why, notwithstanding all the dangers inherent in any local wars or armed conflicts, we cannot but see a fundamental difference between those who fight for freedom and independence and those who seek to retain the colonial order or to impose a new colonial yoke.

We have to draw a clear line and see the difference between the efforts of peoples to achieve national independence, which is quite legitimate and just, and the pretensions of those states or coalitions of states that block the process of national liberation. We must not confuse legitimate self-defense with aggression.

In our day, is the question of who is to blame for wars, the question of who starts military conflicts, canceled? Of course it is not. As applied to wars of national liberation, there is every reason for our having to consider the instigators of military conflicts to be those who obstruct the cause of national liberation. Somerville has said that we should not think that war is the only way to national liberation. One cannot but agree with this. And oppressed people need a destructive war least of all. But who forces them to take up arms and fight a war in which hundreds and thousands of people die and great material values are turned into dust and ashes? If the colonialists and all kinds of international associations of imperialists did not prevent the peoples from exercising their will to live in freedom and independence, then clearly there would be no armed clashes and conflicts. In all these cases, it all ultimately boils down to the fact that the forces that obstruct national liberation and resort to all, including extreme, measures to suppress the national liberation movement are the instigators of so-called local wars and armed conflicts.

Therefore, the acknowledgment of the just nature of the struggle of peoples for their national liberation is not at all a call to war or an encouragement of armed conflicts. This acknowledgment means condemnation of those aggressive forces that impede the national liberation movement. We cannot deny the right of peoples to use armed force against the colonialists for the purpose of achieving free self-determination.

As concerns the threat of a new world war, it goes without saying that the act of unleashing it could not be justified no matter what slogans were used to veil the fact.

But here a question arises: If an aggressive power starts a nuclear war against a peace-loving country that possesses nuclear weapons, can the latter country's use of its nuclear weapons in a war against the aggressor be considered just? And would it not be an encouragement to the aggressor to deny the possibility of a just war against him? There are no answers to these questions in Somerville's speeches.

Science and society should acknowledge that armed aggression—which, as long as nuclear weapons exist, is fraught with the danger of a new world conflict with all its catastrophic consequences—is the most dangerous and unjust form of violating the legal standards of the peaceful coexistence of nations. The state that first uses nuclear, chemical, bacteriological, or other weapons of mass destruction will perpetrate a crime against humanity. Therefore, all active measures on the part of countries subjected to aggression and of all peoples against aggressors should be recognized as just.

Recognition of the just interests of peoples and the legitimacy of their struggle against aggression cannot damage the cause of defending peace. On the contrary, it will help to condemn aggression and isolate the aggressive forces that are, in the final count, the initiators of armed conflicts and wars.

A big contribution to the development of international law would be the recognition of the principle according to which an unjust war is considered an international crime against peace, entailing the culpability of the responsible states and individuals. If we reject the thesis that wars are divisible into just and unjust, then we will weaken our positions in the struggle against aggression and against the supporters of cold war. If we openly condemn aggression as an unjust policy and issue a warning that a war kindled by aggressors will be considered an unjust and criminal war, we will thereby stigmatize all present and future aggressors. By declaring ahead of time that, if they unleash such a war, the struggle of the people in defending themselves will be just and sacred, we will be supporting all who are fighting against an unjust policy today and also against the very possibility of a thermonuclear war breaking out. If we abandon the right to make a distinction between just and unjust wars, we thereby abandon the right to draw a line of distinction between a just and an unjust policy, between a just policy of one class and an unjust policy of another. What we object to is the assertion that in our time, in the age of technology, in view of the danger presented by thermonuclear weapons, we should abandon the positions of Marx and Lenin on just and unjust wars. We pursue our policy in such a way as to avoid a thermonuclear war and to unite all forces on the basis of a just struggle against aggression and for peace among the peoples.

I would like at this point to express a few other ideas. Everyone knows that modern technology, scientific and technological progress, creates weapons of tremendous destructive power. At the same time, it also is important to stress that military production has grown into a gigantic sector of the economy, a vast branch of industry and trade, a vast field that is justifiably called the military-industrial complex. This complex is in the hands of monopoly capital, and in these hands, it represents an extremely dangerous machine. When we say that there are forces in the world that work against a policy of peace and against peaceful coexistence, we have in mind those reactionary circles that feel that war is the only salvation from communism. We must not forget that these people find support precisely in the gigantic military-industrial complex.

Another important aspect of the situation is that the military-industrial complex employs in the production of armaments a huge number of workers, millions of blue- and white-collar workers who are in a privileged position due to the enormous profits made by these industries. This strengthens and reinforces the elements of the so-called workers' and professional aristocracy, which the bourgeoisie uses to stratify and split the working class. That is why the struggle against the military-industrial complex is an important task, part of the struggle for peace. To stem the influence of the military-industrial complex has now become a matter of great social importance.

I would like to add to the foregoing that, despite the resistance of the reactionary forces, we are witnessing a relaxation of international tension. Laboring people in the Soviet Union and in the whole world welcome the favorable changes in the international situation, as it presently exists, in 1973.

How serious is this turn, and how long will it last? To this fundamental question, a question about which millions of people are thinking, a clear-cut and scientifically grounded answer must be given. In such questions of world significance, it is impossible, of course, to define the time limits. But there is every reason to think that it is not a matter of the passing moment, but of a definite, more or less long historical stage in international relations. The point is that the change in world politics was brought about by factors that have been operating for a long time; it is the result of the basic trends of world development. Let us review the main ones.

First, there are the stronger positions of world socialism and all peace-loving forces, the growing influence of the peaceful policy of the Soviet Union and other socialist countries. Dispelled is the myth that the Soviet Union seeks to conquer Europe and the world and to achieve world dominance. No one, apparently, believes this anymore, and even the people who invented this myth now prefer to ignore it in silence.

Second, there is the crisis of imperialist ideology and the policy of force. In the immediate postwar years, one adventuristic concept after another—be it that of containment, of so-called liberation, or of nuclear retaliation—fizzled out. Then about ten or fifteen years ago, they were replaced by the "flexible response" strategy, the most essential element of which was the gamble on "local wars," on destroying the spread of socialism and the national liberation movement by military operations of limited scope. But this tactic, too, turned out to be untenable. After the failure of local wars and military adventures, after the historic victory of the Vietnamese people, after the collapse of the aggression against the Arab states, this policy is no longer considered promising. It is possible that certain forces have not abandoned it completely, but other ways and means in international relations are inevitably being sought, and the principles of peaceful coexistence are receiving ever wider recognition.

Third, there is the sharply intensified craving for peace by the great masses of people, the increased trend in world public opinion toward relaxation of international tension. In fact, the growing burden of military expenditures is increasingly overstraining the economies of the capitalist powers. Militarization of the economy is accompanied now with a greater growth than ever of taxes and inflation. The financial strain develops into a currency crisis. All these factors not only stimulate the growth of antiwar sentiments and movements but also have a sobering influence on a certain number of those political figures who not so long ago saw in international tension and military conflict the means of solving economic and social problems. The main thing is that all social forces and broad democratic movements involved in the struggle for peace, security, and social goals are becoming more and more active. All this is a really powerful factor for peace.

And finally, there are the economic needs, not only in the socialist countries, but also in the capitalist countries, which compel us to search for ways of cooperating in the fields of science and technology and of developing mutually beneficial trade relations. This also is a factor of lasting importance.

That is why we believe that the turn in world politics is not a passing phenomenon. Rather, it is an important historical event. At the same time, however, we have to consolidate our achievements since we cannot regard the improvement of the international situation to be an easy, unimpeded, or automatic process. Many difficulties and obstacles remain along this road. We believe that favorable possibilities and prospects for peaceful coexistence have taken shape, but we must work untiringly to translate them into reality.

* * *

EDITOR'S NOTE

On July 11, 1974, I wrote Academician Professor Fedoseyev as follows: "I am glad to enclose herewith, in accordance with your request, the English translation of your remarks, taken from the tape made by the official translator in Varna. I look forward to receiving from you, as soon as possible, the final version of your report, corrected and supplemented as you wish, for our publication.

"Perhaps I should take this occasion to point out that certain views which you attribute to me on page 3 of the transcript are views which I have never held. I do not reject the thesis of dividing wars into just and unjust. I emphasize the importance of evaluating every war as just or unjust. What I say is that we must include as part of the criteria of a just war the question of the kind of weapons used. That is, it would be impossible to say we are fighting a just war if we use weapons that destroy mankind. Thus, in Cleveland I said: 'But we have lived into a new day in which we must admit that wars fought with the weapons presently available could conceivably destroy the human race, as well as all other living things on the planet Earth, and render this or any similar planet uninhabitable. So we must now face the question: Could any war likely to lead to such a result properly be called a just war?' (p. 5). 'To the extent that any policy, action, strategy or tactic is likely to precipitate thermonuclear war (or any war fought with weapons of similar destructiveness) under the given conditions, it must be judged negatively, and rejected' (p. 6). In Varna I said: 'It is not difficult to see that a central and necessary part of this position of classical Marxism concerning the justification of war was the implicit assumption that the war would not be fought with weapons of total destructiveness, weapons capable, in their technological development, of eliminating all forms of life from the plant Earth' (p. 1). I enclose a copy of these papers in case you do not have the full text of them.''

Before sending me his completed text, Fedoseyev wrote, on September 23, 1974: "In relation to my discussion of your viewpoint, the essential question can be briefly put as follows: If an aggressor starts a nuclear war against a peaceful country which possesses nuclear weapons, is it possible to consider as just the use of nuclear weapons by its side in its war against the aggressor? Also, would not the denial of the possibility of a just war against the aggressor act as an encouragement to his aggression? There is no answer to these questions in the text of your paper. That is what I was referring to.''

On October 10, 1974, I replied to Fedoseyev as follows: "In your letter you ask two questions about my position on the relation between justice and nuclear war. Your first question is: If an aggressive power begins a nuclear war against a peace-loving country which possesses nuclear weapons, may we consider as just the use of nuclear weapons by the peace-loving country in its war against the aggressor? My answer, which I feel sure Marx would agree with, is: Not if such use of nuclear weapons against the aggressor will have the result of exterminating the human race. The destruction of the human future would be the worst of all possible results, the least just.

"We must begin from the premise that, in order to determine the justice or injustice of human actions, not only motives and causes should be taken into account, but consequences and effects. That is, while it is *usually* just for a country to employ, in self-defense, the same kind of weapons with which it has been attacked, this is not *always* just, in light of the consequences. It is not just when the weapons are of the kind which, if used by both sides, will exterminate forever all forms of life, including human life, on the planet Earth.

"This is the case with today's nuclear weapons. The first attack with such weapons will not exterminate the human race. But if that attack is answered by the same kind of weapons, and a series of nuclear exchanges takes place, the human race will be wiped out. I could not characterize such action as just. Human justice always demands that we refrain from actions that will result in the total extermination of the human race even if we have been wronged by others, and our rights have been violated, or unjustly threatened.

"Is not this the principle the Soviet Union actually followed in the Cuban missile crisis? Under the American threat of nuclear bombing of the Soviet missile bases in Cuba, a threat which was aggressive and unjust, the Soviet Union on this occasion gave up its legal right to maintain such bases. Contemporary history shows that the Soviet Union won the immense respect and gratitude of the great majority of people throughout the world by this decision not to defend its rights when such defense would mean a nuclear war which would exterminate humanity.

"In the aftermath of these actual events we can see the answer to your second question: Does this approach, i.e., refusal to enter into nuclear war, encourage the aggressor? The answer is: Yes, it can encourage the aggressor, but this is better than the other result, the total destruction of mankind. We have seen that the same aggressive power was encouraged by the temporary success of its ultimatum in Cuba to make the same aggressive and unjust threats in Vietnam. This is, Nixon set up a mine blockade of Haiphong harbor, and announced he would destroy the ships of any country that tried to enter Vietnamese waters without American permission, specifically mentioning Soviet ships. While the Soviet Union, under this threat of aggressive or nuclear war, gave up its legal right to enter those waters, the ultimate defeat of the aggressor was not thereby prevented. Other ways were found to carry on the war to a victorious conclusion without entering into a nuclear contest that would have destroyed the human race. Surely the possibility will always exist to carry on war without using weapons that annihilate everything, weapons that are unjust precisely because they have that effect.

"Thus my position is that we must always recognize the just or unjust character of every war. A part of this recognition is that a just war will become unjust if it is fought with weapons that exterminate the human race. This is not bourgeois pacifism. It is a demand of Marxist humanism and Marxist dialectics. Having in this way tried to answer the two questions you asked me, may I ask you one question in return? It is this: Do you agree that, if a nuclear reply to a nuclear attack will lead to nuclear exchanges that will exterminate mankind, such a reply would not be just?

"I realize that these are historically new questions of theory and practice, with many complex factors that require much more elaboration and dialogue in order to clarify their content and find satisfactory answers. We will continue to seek answers and to welcome all opportunities of discussion and clarification in order to make every possible contribution to them. I feel this is now more necessary than ever. The dangers are greater now because of the recent changes that have taken place in the context of conditions which surround these questions here."

After receiving Fedoseyev's completed text on October 20, I wrote him as follows:

"Doubtless you have now received the letter I sent you October 10, in which I answered the two questions you raised in your letter of September 23 and which are repeated in your supplemented text. After answering your questions I asked one question of you in return: If the given conditions are such that a nuclear reply by a peace-loving country to a nuclear attack by an aggressor will lead to nuclear exchanges which will exterminate mankind, do you agree that such a reply would be unjust?

"I hope you will wish to add to your supplemented text your reply to this question. I will hold the text and await your reply for inclusion therein because I think these questions and answers are necessary in order to give concrete clarity to our views. In fact, the questions and answers seem to reveal more common ground in relation to our views. For example, you say, 'No sensible person would ever think that a world war might be progressive and just. The only kind of people who could think in terms of a world war are madmen who . . . are afraid of communism more than they are afraid of mankind's destruction' (p. 1). And on p. 4 you say, 'Of course, in these arguments, there is a definite problem connected with the change in the nature of weapons and the probable consequences of a world war in the present epoch.' And on p. 5, 'Somerville has said that we should not think that war is the only way to national liberation. One cannot but agree with this.'

"Unless I misunderstand you, these statements mean that world nuclear war today could destroy mankind, and that such a result would be unjust and mad. But such a result could come about only if the nuclear attacks were answered with nuclear weapons. In that case both sides would be waging war unjustly. Even though the injustice of the aggressor would of course be the greater of the two, the victim also becomes guilty of injustice if he uses the same weapons as the aggressor *when the result of their use by both sides is to destroy mankind*. This is all the more true when it is clear that the aggressor can be fought with weapons that will not result in destroying mankind.

"As I try to understand the relation of your concept of the just war to the question of the destruction of mankind it seems to me you must be making one of two assumptions, both of which are invalid. The first is that the peace-loving country which possesses nuclear weapons could reply to the nuclear attack with its own nuclear weapons in such a way that the resulting nuclear war would not become a world war. Then the destruction might not threaten mankind as a whole. But this assumption that the nuclear war could be confined to the two countries is not in accord with facts, especially when the two countries are 'superpowers.' As we know, each superpower has its camp of friends and allies, East and West around the globe, so that if one of the superpowers becomes involved in war against the other, we must expect that the friends and allies of each will become involved, and that the war will inevitably become a world war. In this connection it is significant that during the Cuban missile crisis both superpowers acknowledged that if they waged nuclear war against each other it would become worldwide, and would destroy mankind. The first assumption is thus invalid on factual grounds.

"The second assumption is that the nuclear war waged by the peace-loving country which had suffered a nuclear attack would still be a just war even though that war would destroy mankind. This would imply a judgment similar to 'better dead than red,' that is, the judgment that it is better to destroy mankind than to allow capitalism to gain a temporary victory. Surely this assumption is equally invalid, on moral grounds. It cannot be just to participate in the destruction of mankind.

"This is how these things appear to me; but perhaps I misunderstand your position, or perhaps I am overlooking something in the objective situation. I would be very grateful for your comment on this.

"As to my own position, please let me say frankly that your formulation of it on p. 4 of your supplemented text still attributes to me views which I do not hold. You say, 'Apparently, Somerville proceeds from the view that since a nuclear world war would now lead to the annihilation of mankind and of all life on Earth, the question of just war is thereby eliminated.' The view I hold is that the question of just wars is thereby modified, not eliminated. I hold that the only thing that is thereby eliminated or outmoded is the old assumption, which was correct enough *in its own time*, that, in deciding whether a given war was just, we did not need to take into account the weapons used, as long as they had been used by the aggressor. That is, the old assumption was that a just war against an aggressor could be fought with any weapons that the aggressor used. This assumption was correct in the nineteenth century because at that time there were no weapons that could destroy mankind in a single war. But now there are, and these weapons create a new and urgent factor in relation to the question of the just war.

"In like manner, my position is misrepresented on p. 7 if you are referring to me when you say, 'If we reject the thesis that wars are divisible into just and unjust. . . .' I must repeat that I do not reject that thesis. On the contrary, I apply that thesis to the question of a nuclear war which can destroy mankind. That is, I hold that a just war can become unjust by waging it with weapons which destroy mankind. If there is a difference between our views it is not that you believe in dividing wars into just and unjust while I do not. It is rather that you believe a just war remains just even when it is waged with weapons that destroy mankind whereas I believe such weapons and such a result would transform the war from just into unjust. In other words, we both divide wars into just and unjust, but possibly we differ about whether a just war can become unjust by the use of certain weapons.

"But perhaps there will be no difference between us on this point when we fully understand each other. I therefore hope that you will reply to my question and comments both for my benefit and the benefit of our readers."

On December 3, 1974, I received the following reply from Fedoseyev: "It seems to me that a prolongation of the discussion of just and unjust wars in relation to a nuclear war that would destroy mankind will lead us into a blind alley and divert us from the main task—from the struggle to prevent such a war. You hold that in the event of a nuclear attack by an imperialist power, a peace-loving socialist country must not have recourse to a nuclear reply because that would also constitute unjust war. In the name of the survival of mankind, the socialist country must agree to the restoration of the capitalist order in the hope of a future liberation through some means other than nuclear weapons. But if we follow this logic, why should the socialist country wait for the nuclear attack with its inevitable mass destruction? Would it not be better to submit in advance to the threat of the aggressor's attack, in order to avoid the mass destruction? But that would not be a philosophy of peace and progress; it would be a philosophy of capitulation to the forces of aggression and reaction.

"Concerning the view that a nuclear reply by the victim of nuclear aggression would inevitably lead to the annihilation of mankind and all life on Earth, it should be noted that this is not the only possible outcome. A nuclear reply, as the just act of a peace-loving power, would naturally be directed at the enemy's nuclear installations; it would in no case be directed against a peaceful population. Of course this would also involve loss of lives. But would it not be logical to suppose that the death-dealing bases of the aggressor would suffer decisive destruction?

"In my opinion, the alternatives are not nuclear destruction of mankind or victory for capitalism, which would be akin to the false demogogic slogan, 'better dead than red.' The idea of exporting communism by force is fundamentally alien to Leninism. But we will not agree to the export to us of counter-revolution under the threat of a nuclear attack.

"However, returning to what I said at the outset, I would like to repeat that our energies should be directed not to working out the rules and moral evaluations of nuclear war, but rather to preventing its possibility, to attaining the permanent prohibition and total destruction of nuclear weapons."

J.S.

3

Human Survival and Soviet Nuclear Policy

SHINGO SHIBATA (Japan)

One somber characteristic of our time, without precedent in the history of the human race, is the possibility that this could very well turn out to be the end of human history, a possibility that appears to be coming closer to materialization. Anyone who rejects this as groundless apprehension should recall a warning given by Bertrand Russell and Albert Einstein, whose sincerity and objectivity cannot be questioned. "The best authorities are unanimous," they declared, "in saying that a war with H-bombs might quite possibly put an end to the human race." And they added, "We have found that the men who know most are the most gloomy."[1] Now, a quarter of a century later, what would Russell and Einstein have to say? The nuclear arms race is accelerating at a rate beyond compare with their days. And what would they say in light of the present buildup of monstrous nuclear weapons, a world system of omnicidal proportions, with such arms deployed everywhere: underground, on the land, under the sea, on the sea, in the air, and in outer space?

Human extinction cannot be considered as just a remote possibility. During the Cuban missile crisis in 1962, the president of the United States took the risk of adopting a policy and putting it into effect, the end result of which he expected would be, as his brother and close adviser during the crisis, Robert Kennedy, expressed it, "the specter of the death of the children of this country [the United States] and all the world, whose lives would be snuffed out like everyone else's."[2] Now the nuclear strategy of the U.S. government has openly gone over to a first-nuclear-strike strategy, which even Senator Barry Goldwater described as too dangerous to be stated publicly, as reported in the *Congressional Record* of June 2, 1975.

Faced by this unprecedented crisis of humanity, however, a growing number of people are taking action throughout the world to free humanity of this threat to their existence. One outstanding action was the International Symposium on the Damage and After-Effects of the Atomic Bombing of Hiroshima and Nagasaki, held in the summer of 1977 in Tokyo, Hiroshima, and Nagasaki, under the auspices of the International Non-Governmental Organizations (NGOs). The symposium proved to be a prelude to a veritable tidal wave of worldwide campaigns for the abolition of nuclear weapons. In May and June of the following year, the United Nations convened its special session devoted to disarmament, the first in its history, for which great credit must go to the initiative of the nonaligned states.

In 1978, addressed to this UN special session devoted to disarmament, 21,178,453 Japanese people affixed their signatures to petitions demanding the abolition of nuclear weapons, and a delegation of more than 500 persons was sent to New York to present the massive volume of signatures to the United Nations.[3] In the United States, there was a rapid growth of the Mobilization for Survival movement, which submitted to President Carter signatures on a petition to outlaw the use of nuclear weapons, and other pressing demands.[4]

The growth of such "mobilization for survival" movements throughout the world was one of the factors that contributed to positive results being achieved by the UN special session on disarmament.

In the first place, the UN special session recognized that mankind is confronted with a crisis that could mean extinction, and that nuclear weapons have to be abolished if human life is to be assured of continued existence. The Final Document adopted by the UN special session devoted to disarmament includes the following statements.

Mankind today is confronted with an unprecedented threat of self-extinction arising from the massive and competitive accumulation of the most destructive weapons ever produced. Existing arsenals of nuclear weapons alone are more than sufficient to destroy all life on this earth.

Removing the threat of a world war—a nuclear war—is the most acute and urgent task of the present day. Mankind is confronted with a choice: we must halt the arms race and proceed to disarmament or face annihilation.

The principal goals of disarmament are to ensure the survival of mankind and to eliminate the danger of war, in particular nuclear war . . . . Effective measures of nuclear disarmament and the prevention of nuclear war have the highest priority. To this end, it is imperative to remove the threat of nuclear weapons, to halt and reverse the nuclear arms race, until the total elimination of nuclear weapons and their delivery systems has been achieved, and to prevent the proliferation of nuclear weapons.

The most effective guarantee against the danger of nuclear war and the use of nuclear weapons is nuclear disarmament and the complete elimination of nuclear weapons.[5]

In the second place, the UN special session resolved that the United Nations should play a central role in bringing about total nuclear disarmament, that the procedures for attaining disarmament should be more democratic, that the Conference of the Committee on Disarmament (CCD), which the two major nuclear powers (the United States and the Soviet Union) had dominated as co-chairmen, had not been effective and should be dissolved, and that in its place a Committee on Disarmament (CD) should be set up, associated more closely with the United Nations, and on which all states should be represented. The Final Document states:

The United Nations, in accordance with the Charter, has the central role and primary responsibility in the sphere of disarmament. Accordingly, it should play a more active role in this field.

All the peoples of the world have a vital interest in the success of disarmament negotiations. Consequently, all States have the duty to contribute to efforts in the field of disarmament. All States have the right to participate in disarmament. All States have the right to participate in disarmament negotiations.

In spite of the best efforts of the international community, adequate results have not been produced with the existing machinery. There is, therefore, an urgent need that existing disarmament machinery be revitalized and forums appropriately constituted for disarmament deliberations and negotiations with a more representative character. For maximum effectiveness, two kinds of bodies are required in the field of disarmament—deliberative and negotiating. All Member States should be represented on the former, whereas the latter, for the sake of convenience, should have a relatively small membership.

The General Assembly establishes as a successor to the Commission originally established by resolution 502 (VI) [of 11 January 1952] a Disarmament Commission composed of all Members of the United Nations.[6]

In the third place, the UN special session confirmed that disarmament, nuclear disarmament in particular, was essential if solutions are to be found to problems facing the developing countries and that the role of the nonaligned states should therefore not be ignored in working for nuclear disarmament. The Final Document places the following emphasis:

In a world of finite resources there is a close relationship between expenditures on armaments and those on economic and social development. Military expenditures are reaching ever higher levels, the highest percentage of which can be attributed to the nuclear-weapons States and most of their allies, with prospects of further expansion and the danger of further increases in the expenditures of other countries. The hundreds of billions of dollars spent annually on the manufacture or improvement of weapons are in somber and dramatic contrast to the want and poverty in which two-thirds of the world's population live. This colossal waste of resources is even more serious in that it diverts to military purposes not only material, but also technical and human resources which are urgently needed for development in all countries, particularly in the developing countries. Thus, the economic and social consequences of the arms race are so detrimental that its continuation is obviously incompatible with the implementation of the new international economic order, based on justice, equity and cooperation. Consequently, resources released as a result of the implementation of disarmament measures should be used in a manner which will help to promote the well-being of all peoples and to improve the economic conditions of the developing countries.[7]

In the fourth place, the UN special session confirmed that not only governments but also the peoples and nongovernmental organizations of the world should play a decisive role in effectuating nuclear disarmament. On this score, the Final Document says:

> It is essential that not only governments but also the peoples of the world recognize and understand the dangers in the present situation. In order that an international conscience may develop and that world public opinion may exercise a positive influence, the United Nations should increase the dissemination of information on the armaments race and disarmament with the full cooperation of Member States.
>
> Throughout this process of disseminating information about the developments in the disarmament field of all countries, there should be increased participation by non-governmental organizations concerned with the matter, through closer liaison between them and the United Nations.
>
> In order to enable the United Nations to continue to fulfil its role in the field of disarmament and to carry out the additional tasks assigned to it by this special session, the United Nations Center for Disarmament should be adequately strengthened and its research and information functions accordingly extended. . . . The Center should also increase contacts with non-governmental organizations and research institutions in view of the valuable role they play in the field of disarmament.[8]

It was in respect of these points that the UN special session on disarmament made an especially positive contribution. Nevertheless, it failed to take such specific steps as would ensure the implementation of these positive points. Of very special importance is the need to outlaw the use of nuclear weapons, but this remains unconfirmed in the Final Document.

In light of paragraph 23 of the Final Document, this omission appears even more strange. It reads:

> Further international action should be taken to prohibit or restrict for humanitarian reasons the use of specific conventional weapons, including those which may be excessively injurious, cause unnecessary suffering or have indiscriminate effects.

Are there any weapons that could more properly be classed as "excessively injurious" or that cause more "unnecessary suffering" or have more "indiscriminate effects" than nuclear weapons? Why were nuclear weapons not included among those weapons that should be eliminated for humanitarian reasons?

It must be said with regret that the UN special session on disarmament, in failing to emphasize the need for a convention outlawing the use of nuclear weapons, failed to follow its own recommendations.

We have noted above both the significance and the limitations of the 1978 UN special session on disarmament. Limitations notwithstanding, the positive significance of that session should by no means be underestimated; it should be used fully in the struggle for human survival.

Of the many tasks that confront mankind at the present time, two should be distinguished as a matter of principle. The first, arising from the fact that humanity and the very possibility of its future could be extinguished, is to rid the world of nuclear weapons once and for all, as a matter of highest priority. The second is how to build a better society for the future, when the future of humanity has been assured. Unless the first undertaking is successful, the second would be futile, no matter how sophisticated the theories and programs that are elaborated.

In considering the first task, it has to be recognized that the governments of the imperialist countries, notably of the United States, have consistently opposed the prohibition and elimination of nuclear weapons and that the arms race has been institutionalized by the U.S. government, whose policy has been a major driving force toward nuclear arms expansion.[9] With this as our premise, it must still be pointed out, as a matter of added significance, that there have been and continue to be serious conflicts among Marxists as to whether the elimination of nuclear weapons should be set as a task, and even if there is agreement that such weapons must be eliminated, the question remains by whom and by what method. In this connection, it cannot be denied that the very advent of nuclear weapons became an important factor contributing to the division among Marxists and within the international Communist movement, which division, of course, has made the elimination of nuclear weapons all the more difficult. In this respect, even after the task of eliminating nuclear weapons was accepted, there have been two basically conflicting policy lines on how and by whom this can be done.[10]

The first of these policy lines, taken by the bloc consisting of the Soviet Union and most of the East European socialist countries (centered in the World Peace Council, although the World Council itself is not a Marxist organization), fundamentally places the two great nuclear powers, the United States and the Soviet Union, in the forefront, attaches major importance to U.S.-Soviet diplomatic negotiations (more exactly, secret diplomacy), and accepts such negotiations as faits accomplis. It is thus big-power centralistic. The method based on this policy line is seen in the Partial Nuclear Test Ban Treaty, signed in 1963 and effective since then; the Nuclear Non-Proliferation Treaty, signed in 1968 and effective since 1970; and more recently by SALT, all characterized by partial, progressive "arms coordination" measures. Protagonists of this line contend that successive partial and progressive measures of arms control (more precisely, "arms coordination") could be expected to lead eventually to the prohibition and elimination of nuclear weapons. Their response is negative toward appealing for the immediate outlawing of the use of nuclear weapons and to the demand for recognizing the right of all states, big and small, to determine this issue.

The second policy line properly places the responsibility of the movement for the elimination of nuclear weapons on the nonaligned countries and the mass movements in the capitalist countries, for whom the nongovernmental organizations speak; it upholds the independence, liberty, equality, and solidarity of all nations based on the principles of nonalignment and the principles of the democratic mass movement. The method to be followed in keeping with this policy line conflicts with the partial and progressive measures and the big-power centralistic "arms coordination" program; it says that the most urgent task of highest priority is to outlaw the use of nuclear weapons under any circumstances whatsoever, by the conclusion of an international treaty to this effect. It is fully committed to "nuclear disarmament," as against "arms coordination," and is the policy advocated and supported by the Japanese peace fighters, including Marxists.

As is well known, the U.S. government, the Japanese government, and the governments of NATO countries, as well as Marxists who stand for the first policy line, have repeatedly branded the second policy line as "unrealistic." The author himself has had the experience at one international conference on nuclear disarmament of hearing Marxists who stood for the first policy line spending most of their time condemning the second policy line as "unrealistic." But when one comes down to realities, only when an agreement outlawing the use of nuclear weapons is concluded can the development, testing, production, stockpiling, and deployment of such weapons become no longer necessary, and the ways leading to the cessation, reduction, and prohibition of the production of such weapons become clear and progressively more concrete. In 1975, according to U.S. data cited in the U.S. Senate, the nuclear arsenals of the United States and the Soviet Union alone held in stock an astronomical volume of destructive power, enough to wipe out all human life twenty-seven times over. In these circumstances, even if the testing of nuclear weapons ceased and production stopped, and even if a treaty were to be signed reducing the existing stockpiles of such weapons by half, the technological "renovation" of missiles and other strategic delivery systems would still be going on, and the crisis of human existence would still have to be overcome, as long as the use of nuclear weapons is not outlawed. These considerations make it clear how unrealistic is the first policy line and how realistic is the second. In view of the grim reality that the series of "partial measures" taken so far have resulted only in the escalation of the nuclear arms race, and in the light of the history and lessons of the movement for the abolition of nuclear weapons and the recommendations of the final document of the 1978 UN special session on disarmament, it cannot be denied that the first policy line has proved to be bankrupt, and even carries within it the danger of the nuclear arms race being further accelerated.[11] It is therefore no exaggeration to say that humanity has no choice but to adopt the second policy line.[12]

In this approach to the goal of nuclear disarmament by way of the second policy line, persistent resistance can be expected not only from the governments of the monopoly capitalist states, the U.S. government in particular, but also from those who stand for the first policy line, represented by the Soviet Union. There are great difficulties also even among those who represent or should represent the second policy line.

In the first place, the Japanese mass movement, one of the major forces among world movements for the abolition of nuclear weapons, was able to collect more than twenty million signatures for submission to the United Nations. Nevertheless, this movement still lacks organizational solidarity and does not constitute a majority in Japan. It has therefore not been successful in winning the Japanese government to its position and in stopping American nuclear weapons from being brought into Japan, nor has the government demanded in the international arena that the use of nuclear weapons be outlawed. The American Mobilization for Survival also is still far from becoming a majority voice in the United States.

Second, while governments of the nonaligned states have proved to be a major force in the promotion of the second policy line, in most of these countries hardly any democratic mass movements have been organized for the elimination of nuclear weapons, and attempts at organizing democratic mass movements as such have mostly been suppressed. Many of these governments are involved in the arms race with conventional weapons, while armed conflicts and hostilities arise among them from time to time, and conventional weapons built up by them have often been turned against their own peoples.

Third, in the advanced capitalist countries of Western Europe, especially in NATO countries, nongovernmental mass movements for the elimination of nuclear weapons have not been organized in strength enough to meet the demands of the situation. In the months leading up to the UN special session on disarmament in 1978, no word was heard from these countries showing any impressive organization of popular movements having taken place, directed specifically to pressuring their respective governments and the United Nations to ban nuclear weapons. The so-called Eurocommunist parties, to the best of my knowledge, did not place adequate importance on the UN special session on disarmament and did not undertake the full organization of mass movements calling for the abolition of nuclear weapons. Even more than that: far from taking the initiative for the elimination of nuclear weapons in the event of a coalition government being established in France, the French Communist party went so far as to advocate the continued possession of nuclear weapons by France.

Fourth, whereas movements for the elimination of nuclear weapons cannot depend for their existence on the governments of the big nuclear powers, but should go on developing as democratic mass movements or nongovernmental organizations, some of these organizations in places other than Japan, the United States, and Western Europe are, in the main, supported financially by their governments. Can such organizations claim to be "nongovernmental"? While the role of nongovernmental organizations is increasing in the United Nations as well as in the organization of international conferences and other forms of action, they in fact include both genuinely nongovernmental organizations supported financially by the masses and de facto "governmental organizations." The latter often play the role of a "speaking tube" for the first policy line and oppose the buildup of democratic mass movements undertaken by genuinely nongovernmental organizations advocating the second policy line.

As we can see from the above account, difficult conditions exist within movements that represent or that should represent the second policy line. It is clear that nuclear weapons cannot be eliminated unless these difficulties are overcome. How fast and on how broad a scale can all the forces working for the elimination of nuclear weapons along the second policy line unite their strength? It would be no exaggeration to say that this will be a major determining factor in deciding whether or not there is a future for humanity.

Even assuming that the above-mentioned difficulties within these movements are overcome and that a convention outlawing the use of nuclear weapons is concluded (such a convention must by all means be concluded, we contend), this convention alone will not guarantee nuclear disarmament or the elimination of nuclear weapons. For nuclear weapons actually to cease to exist, the following minimum problems will have to be solved:

1. How to scrap nuclear weapons under strict international inspection? Specifically, how to control and deal with the uranium and plutonium that will have to be extracted from the vast number of nuclear warheads? They cannot be allowed to be either dumped into the sea or left in deserts as heaps of uranium and plutonium. Simply shouting "No nukes!" will solve nothing. Studies are needed to find out and employ the surest and the most reliable methods of control and disposition.

2. How, under strict international inspection, to control and treat radioactive substances produced in existing nuclear power plants?

3. This raises the problem of how to strengthen the functions of control and inspection to be assumed by the United Nations and by nongovernmental organizations, without infringing on the right of national self-determination. Toward this end, how can the existing principles and machinery of the United Nations, which give the five nuclear powers the right of veto, be democratically renovated, on the principle of equality of nations? Here, the point at issue is five-power centralism and the existing principles and machinery of the United Nations, which will have to be rebuilt.

4. How to anticipate and overcome the obstinate resistance of, or even an attempted coup by, the military of big imperialist nuclear powers?

5. In the event of nuclear weapons actually being scrapped, an unprecedented depression could be expected to result from the breakdown of monopoly capital in the arms industry that has produced such weapons, in American state monopoly capitalism, and in world capitalism in general. How can unemployment be prevented from expanding seriously, with medium and minor firms going bankrupt and with the people's livelihood being ruined? How can democratic control be instituted over munitions monopoly capital? How can the munitions economy be converted to a peace economy? How can the political and military machinery standing in the way of conversion be democratically regulated?

6. How to work out a democratic economic program, a program for the development of resources and energy, a program for the progress of science and technology, and a program for peace education—programs that would make the preceding undertakings possible? How to establish a people's majority and form a consensus both at national and at international levels?

7. How to dismantle nuclear-capable military blocs and and bases and bring these things under international and democratic supervision?

These are but some of the tasks that must certainly be faced, along with many others that will have to be tackled. What is already clear, taking all into consideration, is that unless these problems, stated as a minimum, are solved, humanity can never be freed of nuclear weapons (the world system of omnicidal instruments). On the contrary, all mankind, including Marxists, the existing socialist countries, and their peoples, will continue to face the possibility of extermination.

As far as this writer knows, not only Marxists of the Soviet Union and the East European countries but also Eurocommunist theorists, far from having solved them, have yet to set themselves to these tasks. Needless to say, neither Marx, Engels, Lenin, nor Gramsci was able to foresee the possibility of the ending of world history by means of nuclear weapons. It is a qualitatively new situation, and some of the propositions advanced by classical Marxism now have to be reexamined and, if need be, rectified in the light of this.[13]

The task of eliminating nuclear weapons to ensure human survival is more than just one among many tasks confronting humanity. It constitutes a major condition which, if not fulfilled, will bring to naught all other objectives. It is our greatest task. Only by fulfilling it, can the way toward democracy and the antimonopoly revolution in advanced countries be cleared, in order to make possible the transition to socialism. Only thus can the difficulties faced by the nonaligned countries (developing countries) as well as by the present socialist countries (backward socialist countries) be overcome. In other words, the successful carrying out of this task is the only guarantee of a future for the human race. It is thus the central and most important task affecting the whole destiny of humanity, which, in turn, will make possible the completion of the second task, that of building a better future.

NOTES

1. Bertrand Russell and Albert Einstein, "Manifesto," 1955.
2. See Robert F. Kennedy, *Thirteen Days: A Memoir of the Cuban Missile Crisis* (New York: New American Library, 1969), p. 106. For a discussion of the most serious implications of President John F. Kennedy's policy during the Cuban missile crisis, see John Somerville, *The Peace Revolution* (Westport, Conn., and London, England: Greenwood Press, 1975).
3. The wording of the petitions was as follows:

So that there will be no more hibakusha [victims of the atomic bombs], and in order to build a peaceful world without nuclear weapons;
We request the following of the United Nations:

*to make known to the people of the world the horrors of the Hiroshima-Nagasaki atomic bombing and the sufferings of the hibakusha;
*to outlaw the use of nuclear weapons as a crime against humanity;
*to hold a world disarmament conference, and as soon as possible to make treaties completely prohibiting the use, testing, manufacture, stockpiling, proliferation and deployment of nuclear weapons.

4. "A petition to President Jimmy Carter on the occasion of the Special Session on Disarmament of the United Nations," drafted and sponsored by the American Mobilization for Survival, reads:

Mr. President, fulfill your campaign pledges. Cut military spending. Move toward a world of *zero* nuclear weapons.
1. RESOLVE to join other nations in outlawing the use of nuclear weaponry as a crime against humanity.
2. PLEDGE that under no circumstances would the U.S. be the first to use nuclear weapons.
3. END all research, development, testing, production and deployment of nuclear weapons and launching systems, including the neutron bomb, the cruise missile, the M-X missile and the Trident submarine.
4. INITIATE major reductions of our nuclear weapons stockpile.
5. STOP the export of nuclear technology and actively pursue development of non-nuclear energy sources at home and abroad.
6. HALT all arms sales abroad—especially the sale of conventional weapons to dictatorial and repressive regimes.
7. CUT the military budget by 15% this year and shift the money into areas of human need.
8. GUARANTEE decent and productive jobs for those now employed in military and nuclear industries.

Mr. President, these are eight immediate *initiatives toward* complete and general disarmament that our country can take without risk to our security. They would spur other nuclear powers to take similar action. People of the world are waiting for some nation to take the first step—let it be us.

5. U.N. Special Session on Disarmament, Final Document, paragraphs 11, 18, 19-20, 56.
6. Ibid., paragraphs 114, 28, 113, 118.
7. Ibid., paragraph 16.
8. Ibid., paragraphs 15, 104, 123.
9. In this connection, it is noteworthy that NATO opened its session on May 30, 1978, in Washington, D.C., at the very same time as the U.N. special session on disarmament was meeting in New York. President Carter addressed the opening ceremony of the Washington meeting, stressing the need for strengthening and modernizing the NATO forces (e.g., with neutron bombs). Following the opening ceremony, full-scale deliberations took place behind closed doors in the Department of State. The NATO session confirmed that military expenditures of the NATO countries for 1979-84 would be increased by 3 percent annually. It also approved a total of 117 recommendations that included, among others, measures for: (1) strengthening a combat-ready system capable of deploying armed forces at any time and at any place around the globe; (2) increasing the offensive power of air forces; and (3) updating nuclear weapons. This NATO session again revealed the dangerous and provo-

cative stance of the highest officials of NATO governments, led by the United States.

10. The Government of the People's Republic of China had once stood for a correct position in advocating the convocation of a world summit conference to be participated in by all states, not just by nuclear powers, for the purpose of achieving the total elimination of nuclear weapons. From about the mid-1960s, however, the Chinese leadership began a backward shift of its nuclear policy and switched to a position antagonistic to the world peoples' movements for the eradication of nuclear weapons. From the early 1970s, the Chinese began to follow U.S. global policy, and went so far as to encourage the most reactionary, corrupt, fascist regimes throughout the world. Actions show the present Chinese leadership to be neither Marxist nor socialist, but big-power hegemonist and social imperialist.

11. For elucidation of the arms control negotiations by the two great nuclear powers, the United States and the Soviet Union, standing in the way of achieving genuine nuclear disarmament, see Alva Myrdal, *The Game of Disarmament: How the United States and Russia Run the Arms Race* (New York: Pantheon Books, 1976). For a discussion of the true nature of SALT, see Barton J. Bernstein, "SALT: The Dangerous Illussion," *Inquiry*, July 24, 1978.

12. As can be seen from the demands quoted in notes 3 and 4 above, the nongovernmental mass movements in Japan and the United States have no illusions whatsoever about arms control and SALT as subscribed to by the United States and the Soviet Union. These movements have sternly denounced the nuclear policies followed by their respective governments and have taken an independent position, differing from the policies of the Soviet government and of the World Peace Council. No grass-roots organization in Japan has ever placed its hopes in the outcome of SALT.

13. Although Marx, Engels, and Lenin argued that technological development under capitalism and imperialism would be accompanied by great suffering and loss of human resources, they could not foresee that such would become so serious as to mean human extinction. Today, however, we are faced by two possibilities. One is the possibility of human extinction that could mean the end of world history, and the other is the possibility of humanity overcoming this crisis so that it can move from capitalism to socialism. Not only as a Marxist but also as a member of the human family, the writer is of course eager to see that the latter possibility is brought to reality, although the existence of the former cannot be denied. The danger of this former possibility should

be brought home to everyone, and all-out efforts should be made to prevent it. In so doing, Marxists should vigorously seek a path of cooperation with non-Marxists, for the task of preventing mankind from destroying itself cannot be fulfilled by Marxists and socialists alone. It can be done only with the participation of all members of the human family. For all humanity to take part in this "mobilization for survival," such thoughts and theories as will make this process possible should be formulated and promulgated, including in particular the reconstruction of the theories of fundamental human rights and modern democracy, theories that are most fitted to this new situation.

A reevaluation of various political and ideological positions of different schools of social science, of manifold styles in the arts, and of a wide range of religious teachings also is needed, a reevaluation in terms of the prevention of human extinction so that all such can find their own proper places in the "mobilization for survival" movement.

On problems posed to Marxism by the human extinction crisis, John Somerville's book cited in note 2 above is a pioneering work. In *'Eurocommunism' and the State* (London: Hill, 1977), S. Carrillo, secretary-general of the Communist party of Spain, argues that because of the advent of nuclear weapons, some of the Marxist positions—the thesis, for instance, that war is the continuation of politics by other means—should be rectified. He quotes Marx:

> . . . proletarian revolutions . . . criticise themselves constantly, interrupt themselves continuously in their own course, come back to the apparently accomplished in order to begin it afresh, deride with unmerciful thoroughness the inadequacies, weaknesses and paltrinesses of their first attempts. (Marx, *The Eighteenth Brumaire of Louis Bonaparte*, in: Marx/Engels, *Selected Works*, London: International, 1968, p. 98).

From such a standpoint, Carrillo points out that we must recognize that there exists "a Marxist, revolutionary *revisionism*" and that Lenin *revised* certain theses of Marx revolutionarily.

In this work, Carrillo presents problems quite challenging to the traditional Marxist way of thinking; it is a work that is to be valued positively in many respects. However, Carrillo says that nuclear weapons have so far acted as a "nuclear deterrent" and that "nuclear deterrent strategy" and an equilibrium of nuclear military power between the United States and the Soviet Union have advanced coexistence between the two powers. If such a distinguished Marxist as Carrillo holds this untenable conception of "nuclear deterrent strategy," the

Japanese movement for the elimination of nuclear weapons will be seen to have greater significance, and Japanese Marxism a greater international role. Of themes that need to be examined and studied from the Marxist standpoint or that demand that Marxism reexamine some of its own positions, the following can be pointed out:

Do "socialist countries," by reason of their character, pursue "general and complete disarmament"? Why has the Soviet Union regressed in its nuclear policy from "elimination of nuclear weapons" to "control of nuclear arms"? Why does the Soviet Union stand for the clearly weaker policy line and resist the much stronger policy line? Why has "bigpower nationalism" emerged in the Soviet Union and China, and not been overcome? What attitude should Marxists take toward the policy of developing nuclear weapons in "socialist countries" that adopt such a policy? How should the movement for nonalignment be defined from the standpoint of the worldwide class struggle? Why is the movement for nonalignment more progressive than that of "socialist countries" in the struggle for the elimination of nuclear weapons? How should the present United Nations and a democratically renovated United Nations be defined in light of the Marxist theory of the state? How can the international inspection to be undertaken by the United Nations be made compatible with the principle of the right to national self-determination? How should the nongovernmental movement be defined in light of Marxist theories of mass movements, of united fronts, and of the class struggle? What new problems has the nongovernmental movement presented to Marxism? What problems have been posed by the movement for the eradication of nuclear weapons to the theory of revolution in advanced countries? While nuclear disarmament is a categorical imperative, is so-called general and complete disarmament (in which the elimination of conventional weapons is included) feasible before the accomplishment of Socialist revolution on a worldwide scale, including the revolution in advanced countries, and before the withering away of states? If such general and complete disarmament is not practicable, should it be rejected as an illusory slogan? If it is to be pursued as a practicable task, should some of the propositions advanced by the Marxist theory of the state be rectified? Is it possible for nongovernmental organizations in socialist countries to continue their existence even when their positions are different from those of their respective governments? If they cannot exist under such circumstances, is it possible to speak of the nongovernmental movement in socialist countries? All these questions need to be answered in light of the present new situation.

Another question that needs to be addressed is the history of Soviet nuclear policy. When U.S. imperialism proposed nuclear arms *control*, in 1946, the Soviet Union resolutely opposed this and proposed the *prohibition* and *elimination* of nuclear weapons. The Soviet Union at that time proposed a convention for the absolute prohibition of the use of atomic weapons and a designation of the breach of the convention as a crime against humanity, with severe penalties for any breach, together with application of the convention to all nations. These were just and principled proposals. From that time and up to June 1954, the Soviet Union consistently demanded, both in the United Nations and at the level of the mass movement, that nuclear weapons be prohibited. This policy was in conformity with the demand made by the movement for the prohibition of atomic and hydrogen bombs organized among the peoples of the world, in which the Soviet Union was able to claim legitimate prestige. In opposition to this policy of the Soviet Union and the worldwide movement demanding the prohibition of nuclear weapons, the governments of the United States and the NATO countries consistently opposed the prohibition of such weapons and put forward arms control plans and progressive disarmament proposals.

But suddenly, in September 1954, the Soviet Union made a big retreat from its former position. It accepted as a basis of discussion the principle of progressive disarmament proposals, which had been submitted in June of that year by the United Kingdom and France, and declared at a session of the UN General Assembly that it was prepared to drop the demand for the immediate prohibition of nuclear weapons. In May 1955, the Soviet Union made very comprehensive disarmament proposals, which were closer to the Western proposals and oriented to phased disarmament and arms control, but did not include as the immediate aim the prohibition of nuclear weapons.

At the level of the movement for the prohibition of nuclear weapons after 1954, only the prohibition of nuclear test explosions was made a major issue, not the prohibition of nuclear weapons themselves. This was partly because the consciousness of the peoples of the world was not mature enough, a condition for which the Soviet Union was not solely responsible. In November 1956, the Soviet Union justly denounced the United Kingdom and France for their aggression against Egypt and even implied the possibility of using nuclear weapons against the aggressors. As a result, the Anglo-French partners ceased their aggression against Egypt, but the fact remains that the Soviet Union used the threat of nuclear weapons as an instrument of pressure. Since 1957, the Soviet Union has made one proposal after another for partial arms control and for the cessation of nuclear tests, and in September 1959 presented proposals for general and complete disarmament, moved by Premier Khrushchev at the United Nations. The urgent demand for the prohibition of nuclear weapons was carefully dropped, with sharper attention paid to problems of partial arms control and the ending of nuclear tests, which would not necessarily lead to the prohibition of nuclear weapons. At the same time, an all-out effort was made to create illusions about a rose-colored general and complete disarmament, which would surely not be feasible for a long time.

Thus, Soviet nuclear policy after September 1954 marked a retreat from the demand for the prohibition and elimination of nuclear weapons to the position of nuclear arms control, moving actually closer to the Baruch plan. This retreat was combined with a big-power-centered policy of removing "disarmament" problems from the purview of the United Nations, so as to deal with them by way of diplomatic negotiations between the two major powers, the United States and the Soviet Union. The tendency was thus strengthened, not for the United Nations to regulate the nuclear arms expansion race under the influence of the United States and the Soviet Union, but for these two major nuclear powers to regulate the United Nations by presenting as a fait accompli the results of their own diplomatic negotiations. From this came the policy of big-power intervention, which attempted to impose this same fait accompli on the world movement for the prohibition of nuclear weapons, and on Japan in particular, where the Soviet Union tried to transform the movement into one of support for its own nuclear policy. This was one factor among others that in 1964 caused the split in the Japanese movement for the prohibition of nuclear weapons. In this way, the policy line came into being, oriented to partial and phased arms coordination measures of big-power centralism. This policy revealed itself as incapable of regulating the U.S. imperialist policy of nuclear arms expansion, and contributed to the establishment of a series of arms control treaties sanctioned by U.S. imperialism, beginning with the 1963 partial nuclear test ban treaty.

What is the present Soviet nuclear policy? What steps has the Soviet leadership proposed for the elimination of nuclear weapons? Such steps can be summed up from the speech by L. I. Brezhnev on November 2, 1977. He proposed: (1) that the approximate equilibrium of military power existing between the Soviet Union and the United States be maintained; (2) that a downward turn in the curve of the arms race be started [which allows that the curve could also go up—S.S.]; (3) that the level of military confrontation be gradually scaled down; (4) that as "a radical step," an agreement on a simultaneous halt in the production of nuclear weapons be reached by all states; (5) that the existing stockpiles of nuclear weapons be reduced, to be followed by their complete and total destruction; and (6) that an agreement on a moratorium covering nuclear explosions for peaceful purposes be concluded, along with a ban on all nuclear weapons tests for a definite period.

In light of the emphasis placed on proposed steps (4) and (6), it is clear that the Soviet leadership for the present time at least is not making the total prohibition of nuclear weapons the aim of struggle. It also is clear that these form part of the policy of nuclear arms control, premised on a nuclear deterrent strategy and not a policy for the prohibition or elimination of nuclear weapons.

In contrast, what is the policy of the nongovernmental movement in Japan and elsewhere on the prohibition and elimination of nuclear weapons? As I understand it, the principles and steps commonly confirmed in the nongovernmental movement in Japan against nuclear weapons may be summed up as:

1. To provide relief and assistance to *hibakusha*, the surviving victims of the first nuclear war, and to have the Japanese government enact a genuine "hibakusha relief law." To disseminate authentic information on the damage and sufferings caused by the first atomic bombing, or, more precisely, the first act of nuclear omnicide, to warn the world against, and do our utmost to prevent, further acts of nuclear omnicide.

2. To work for conclusion of a treaty banning the use of nuclear weapons, mainly through the medium of the United Nations, with all states parties to it. To have the Japanese government enact and implement a law embodying the three nonnuclear principles (not to produce, not to possess, and not to bring in nuclear weapons). To internationalize these three nonnuclear principles and, specifically, to expand nuclear-free zones.

3. To have all nuclear weapons scrapped, under a plan in which all states cooperate, under United Nations control. The steps leading to the general and complete elimination of nuclear weapons should include specifically; (a) the prohibition of tests, manufacture, stockpiling, and deployment of nuclear weapons; (b) the reduction and complete elimination of nuclear weapons; and (c) the control by the United Nations of all fissionable source materials.

4. Such steps should be followed by disarmament in relation to conventional arms, i.e., general and complete disarmament.

To realize these steps, it is necessary to have a nonsectarian, united mass movement developed on the widest possible scale. Such a mass movement should unite precisely for the attainment of these objectives, and the question of whether or not support should be given to a certain diplomatic policy, or to a certain nuclear policy or "partial measures" relating to nuclear weapons adopted by any government or governments, can never be made a required tenet of belief for such a movement, or even be brought into it. Independent and self-determined unity of the movement based on agreed aims for relief of *hibakusha* and for the prohibition and elimination of nuclear weapons should be the organizational principle of nongovernment movements for the prohibition of nuclear weapons in Japan and elsewhere.

4
Nuclear Weapons, World Peace, and Contemporary Marxism

DEBIPRASAD CHATTOPADHYAYA (India)

After I received an advance copy of John Somerville's paper, I took the initiative of organizing a seminar in Calcutta, where about twenty-one Marxist scholars were present, to discuss his paper. I have a list of these scholars that I would like to make available to Professor Somerville. I also have a printed copy of my paper, which actually is based on the discussions we had in the seminar. I refer to these because it is not my views alone that I am going to air here. It is a kind of collective view of our theoreticians in Calcutta.

The first effect of Somerville's paper has been frankly stunning. Not that we cannot recall those grim and anxious days through which we had to pass during the Cuban missile crisis. But that was a decade back. What has in the meanwhile reached us is mainly the stream of cheerful news about the growing happiness of the Cuban people under conditions of freedom for which they fought and which they won. To us, therefore, the crisis is a matter of the past. It belongs to a dusty little cupboard more or less forgotten. However, with the keys that he took from Robert Kennedy's posthumous publication, Somerville opens the cupboard, from which he drags out a skeleton—a skeleton that has an awful story to tell. In sheer horror, it is in fact more awful than any story ever told. During the Cuban missile crisis, the American government's policymaking process reached a decision according to which the total destruction of the human race was deliberately chosen in preference to a simultaneous removal of Soviet missiles from Cuba and American missiles from Turkey. For this total annihilation, Robert Kennedy used the rather casual expression "snuffing out."

That such a decision could be taken—and, as a matter of fact, was taken—is stunning. It surpasses credulity if for no other reason than its appalling criminality. Yet Somerville documents it so satisfactorily that even without going through Kennedy's book one is left with little ground to doubt.

Somerville mentions this to focus on one question: How would Marx have faced such a situation? This means, when imperialism gets prepared to commit even such a crime, what is the contemporary Marxist—or, more specifically, the socialist world under the leadership of the Soviet Union—going to do? The question is much more difficult than the older one of fighting a war with conventional weapons. In the context of the contemporary revolution in science and technology, conventional weapons have become largely obsolete. A decisive global war today, if fought at all, will be fought ultimately with remote-controlled thermonuclear warheads, against the massive use of which there is really no effective defense. Such a war cannot end in victory for anyone because it is bound to annihilate all. Thus, Somerville feels, along with the conventional weapons, the older concept of a just war in defense of human right has become obsolete. A global war today is not going to leave any human beings behind, whose right it may be imagined to defend. And the fact is that the policy-forming process of the American government is capable of committing itself to such a war. What then are Marxists going to do? How are socialists going to face the situation?

The question is evidently too momentous to be answered in haste. What we can perhaps try to have are some clarifications.

The first clarification I am myself anxious to have is on a counterquestion: What are the capitalists going to do about it? How are they going to face the situation? The answer that Robert Kennedy's book is there to see it, does not appear to be adequate. Certain figures before me raise further questions. The financial oligarchy that controls the largest monopolies of America today consists of about 5,000 persons. In 1968, there were about 200,000 persons in the United States whose private fortunes exceeded $1 million each. I have no figures about the millionaires in Japan, West Germany, Great Britain, France, and so forth. But that does not so much matter, for I can easily presume that their total number must be fairly high. And my question is: What do all these people really feel, and what are they going to do when there is the proposal of "snuffing out" everybody, i.e., inclusive of themselves and their relations? Apparently, none can believe that the contemporary revolution in science and technology, however spectacular it may be, has any trick to exempt the capitalists from the wholesale murder of humankind in the nuclear holocaust. Cuba, I know, is extremely distasteful to them; so is the very existence of a rival world socialist system. Their eagerness and anxiety to mop these up are understood. What is not understood, however, is their own readiness to be themselves mopped up in the process. Or are they really capable of thinking in terms of a future dead world in which their balance sheets lie buried under the corpses of both the socialists and the capitalists? I cannot but wonder!

Robert Kennedy said that while making this decision to end the world what disturbed the American president most was the "spectre of the death of the children of this country and all the world." Let us hope that this at least is true, that it was not meant to be a Hollywood touch to soften up the effect of the diabolical decision. But, then, the president evidently thought of the wrong persons, for the children had nothing to do with the setting up of the American decision-making power. A more realistic thought would have been about the American oligarchy —primarily those 5,000 persons who control the monopolies, although perhaps secondarily also of those 200,000 millionaires. These are the persons to whom America's decision-making process ultimately owes its own existence and its own strength. This point is indeed so well known that it is hardly necessary to argue it over again. In the present context, however, it may be useful to reiterate the main facts. As it is aptly put, although democratic in form, the American government is actually plutocratic in content. Votes are only the nominal sources of the political power, its real source being money—lots and lots of money, real big money—which is required for indoctrinating the voters, organizing the electoral campaigns, maintaining the political parties, not to speak of doing the kinds of things that have caused the recent huge scandals. Since this big money can come only from those that possess it, they are the real sources of the political power.

All these facts are so palpable today that one need not be a Marxist to see them. That is why I feel all the more bothered by my question. Are the 5,000 men controlling the monopolies fully aware of the fact that the power set up by their money did in 1962 make a decision that amounted to a proposal of liquidating their very existence? Are the 200,000 millionaires aware of it? If so, what are they going to do about it? How are they going to face the situation?

I could have extended my question to the capitalists of the other parts of the world. But I have more important persons to think of. In the United States, the 200,000 millionaires make up only 0.25 percent of the working population. They are the direct voters after all. Are they aware that, since the decision was once made to snuff them out, there is the danger of it being repeated? Perhaps they are really not aware of this. But if they are not, they have got to be told about it, so that while casting their next vote they can think twice. It may be that there is something for them to do even before casting the next vote. But they must know the truth first.

I can readily presume that it is not easy to tell all these things to the American working class. But then I also am aware that the American intellectuals are increasingly realizing their responsibility to tell the truth to the American people. What was once just a ripple of protest against the Vietnam war eventually assumed the form of a massive movement. Hence, I do not despair. How can I despair when I see that a leading philosopher of America today, Noam Chomsky, defies the most gigantic propaganda machine, and dedicates his book, *The New Mandarins*, "To those brave young men who refuse to serve in a criminal war"?

Much, therefore, depends on the philosophers or, more broadly on the intellectuals, who are supposed to be able to see what is going on beneath the surface. They are supposed to have the right equipment for analyzing facts. What they need more of is the courage to communicate. This courage they have got to gather. The alternative is to wait and perish.

Let me try to be clearer about what I am saying. I am not talking of possible nuclear retaliation by the socialist world. Retaliation or no retaliation, if imperialism unleashes a nuclear war, we all perish. Let us imagine a situation in which the Soviet Union remains firm with a holy resolve never to touch these unholy weapons, and allows imperialism systematically to annihilate with nuclear weapons all the important cities, industries, bases, and so forth, from Tashkent to Tbilisi, and also all those in East Germany, Hungary, Poland, Bulgaria—everywhere in the socialist world. What is going to happen then? All the peoples in the socialist world die, of course. But that is not all. All the peoples of the capitalist world as well as all the peoples in the third world also die, and this regardless of any nuclear retaliation by the socialists. Here is only one reason for this.

It is for the experts to calculate how many megatons of nuclear warheads will have to be exploded for such a systematic annihilation. Those who are capable of making this calculation should be able to calculate also the amount of radiostrontium that will have to be committed to the stratosphere for the purpose and on what near future that is going to come down on us all as our slow but sure doom. Here is an account of this cancer-causing agent already in the sky, which I quote from Robert Jungk:

> The American physicist Ralph Lapp uttered an even more serious warning, based on conversations with an Atomic Energy Commission biologist who would not allow publication of his name for fear of dismissal. Lapp stated: "In 1945 55,000 tons of TNT equivalent were detonated. Sporadic testing followed until the tentacles of the cold war gripped the nation and the test rate zoomed up. My calculations show that if the world does follow the test schedule I have assumed, by 1962 there will be an amount of radiostrontium committed to the stratosphere which sometime in the 1970s will add up to the *maximum possible amount* for the world's population. Just what do we mean by the maximum possible amount of a radioactive substance?

Will more than this amount cause illness or death? If so, how much more? Is it safe for all humans to have one maximum possible amount of strontium retained in their bones? All maximum possible amount limits in the past have been specified for small groups of healthy adults working under controlled conditions and exposed to known hazards. . . . Therefore most experts believe that the maximum possible amount for whole populations should be ten times less than the occupational level."[1]

Thus, the risk we are already exposed to is more than alarming. Deliberately going in for a greater risk is out of the question.

Whether the socialists retaliate or not, the nuclear weapons themselves are going to retaliate. In other words, the contemporary revolution in science and technology is not to be superficially understood. It might have created the possibility of destruction in a scale hitherto undreamed of. But this destructiveness is too fantastic, too colossal, too all-absorbing to be put in actual practice. It harbors within itself its opposite, namely, a definite deterrent against its massive use. I want to emphasize the words "massive use" because P. M. S. Blackett has already argued why, militarily speaking, the American use of nuclear weapons against the Soviet Union will be really useless, unless these are used on a very massive scale.[2]

If, therefore, we are to believe that a decision was actually made for the massive use of these weapons, it appears to us to have been something like a drunken decision—or a temporary insanity—that even the capitalists would have hardly allowed to be fully implemented, but which in any case the Soviet Union allowed to cool off by withdrawing its missiles unilaterally.

This leads us to see the kind of weapon the Soviet Union is actually interested in using against imperialism. Not that the Soviet Union does not possess nuclear weapons of its own. After all, it would be crazy to be without a gun when you know that there is a gunman about. No one expects the socialist world to overlook the network of military bases and the many pacts that add to the already existing ones encircling the entire socialist world. Even the somewhat dated figures make us stagger. "In 1959, the United States had, according to Fleming, a total of 275 major base complexes in 31 countries and more than 1,400 foreign bases, counting all sites where Americans were then stationed, and sites designed for emergency occupation."[3] While nuclear weapons are being piled up in those bases, how can the socialist world totally ignore them?

But the mere fact of possessing nuclear weapons does not mean one is anxious to use them—no more than the mere possession of a gun against the gunman means an actual interest in a shooting spree. Whatever fiction the paperbacks may have to tell, the fact is that the socialist world never showed any interest in the actual use of nuclear weapons even in moments of grave provocation, like those of the Cuban missile crisis. It has not shown this interest because it does not need to; it does not need to because it has in its armory a weapon much more devastating for imperialism. It is the weapon of world peace. I need not quote here the policy statements by the socialist leaders to prove this, for there are accredited American admissions proving it. I quote one of these. William S. Schlamm, the former editor of *Fortune*, emphatically asserted: "Communism *thrives* on peace, *wants* peace, *triumphs* in peace."[4] Mr. Schlamm, it needs to be noted, is not a socialist. What annoys him most is the presence of the Russians in Eastern Europe. He advocates nuclear ultimatums to get them out.

What is it in world peace that gives so much power to socialism? How is it that peace hurts imperialism and hurts it badly? The answer is that imperialism wants to thrive on war, wants war, dreams of triumphing in war.

I have before me an excellent book called *Monopoly Capital: An Essay on the American Economic and Social Order*, by Paul A. Baran and Paul M. Sweezy.[5] By an impassioned analysis of this order, well backed up by statistical data, the authors show that, given this order, there is a definite limit beyond which the productive power ushered in by the contemporary revolution in science and technology cannot be used for civilian purposes, such as for health, housing, education, and food. The authors show "how in case after case the private interests of the oligarchy stand in stark opposition to the satisfaction of social needs."[6] One alternative for this order, therefore, is to keep both men and machines idle and to force this idleness to coexist with deprivation at home and starvation abroad.

Thus rebuffed by the prospect of serving civilian purposes, this economic and social order finds itself increasingly committed to the other alternative, which, basically speaking, is that of converting the forces of production into forces of destruction. "On what could the government spend enough to keep the system from sinking into the mire of stagnation? On arms, more arms and ever more arms."[7]

I do not have the scope here to go into all the details. But here is how one of the most eminent scientists of our time sums up the situation: "It is the same demand for maximum profit that has given in recent years the heavy bias of technology and science towards military uses. Profits there are enormous; the public pays without asking awkward questions, and the resulting goods do not clog the market. They can be expended in wars or, if that fails, scrapped in a few years as obsolete. The demand for them is also reinforced by every means of propaganda needed to keep up war fever and justify military expenditure."[8] Since World War II, the place of the monopolists is taken up by the government. "This new arrangement, which operates in Britain as well as America, is that of the research and development contract, almost exclusively for war material. It has proved very convenient for monopoly firms, as the government pays the costs and takes all the risks, while, once in production, industry takes all the profits."[9]

That this is no exaggeration can be easily seen from certain American opinions on the immense profitability of war preparations expressed with brutal candor. Here are some of these:

U.S. News & World Report observed, "Government planners figure they have found the magic formula for almost endless good times. . . . Cold War is the catalyst. Cold War is an automatic pump primer. Turn a spigot, the public clamors for more arms spending. Turn another, the clamor ceases. . . . Cold War demands, if fully exploited, are almost endless."[10]

In 1954, the same periodical commented on the successful explosion of an H-bomb by America: "What H-bomb means to business. A long period of big orders. In the years ahead, the effects of the new bomb will keep on increasing. As one appraiser put it, "The H-bomb has blown depression-thinking out of the window.' "[11]

The Cold War, explained a Harvard economist, "increases the demand for goods, helps sustain a high level of employment, accelerates technical progress and thus helps the country to raise its standard of living."[12]

Senator Proxmire spoke from his own experience: "Programs that wouldn't get a second look from Congress flit through if they are attached to an armed forces appropriation."[13]

The experience of Senator Russell, recounted by himself, is an even more devastating condemnation of the entire system: "There is something about preparing for destruction that causes men to be more careless in spending money than they would be if they were building for constructive purposes. Why that is so, I do not know; but I have observed, over a period of almost thirty years in the Senate, that there is something about buying arms with which to kill, to destroy, to wipe out cities, and to obliterate great transportation systems which causes men not to reckon the dollar cost as closely as they do when they think about proper housing and the health of human beings."[14]

Those who are interested in more admissions like these may look into Baran and Sweezy's book. However, what is necessary for understanding our present point is already obvious. If capitalism wants to survive ultimately by converting its productive forces into the forces of destruction, what hits it hardest is world peace. Thus, there is really no mystery about peace becoming such a powerful weapon for socialism in the world today. It destroys the last hope of capitalism and thus leaves it to face its own impending doom.

But there is more. World peace enables socialism to show in the form of concrete historical examples what the same revolution in science and technology can positively ensure for human beings today. It can ensure energy in practically unlimited quantity; it can ensure the possibility of relegating the drudgery of manual and even clerical labor mainly to machines; it can ensure the understanding and therefore the mastery of the biological process on a deeper level. In other words, the peaceful application of the same revolution in science and technology can stamp out the objective justification for all forms of poverty, slavery, and deprivation. And this socialism alone can demonstrate. That, again hurts imperialism, for imperialism wants people to see in this revolution only the horrors of the fission and fusion bombs, the remote control of long-distance missiles, and the lethal biological pile—in short, only the messengers of death.

Thus, the contemporary revolution in science and technology is not a thing-in-itself. Whether it is going to mean life or death depends on the economic and social content within which it is placed. This social order, again, is not a deity toying with human fate. It is for human beings to choose it. Millions of men and women in the socialist world have already made their choice. it now remains for the toiling millions in the capitalist world as well as in the third world to make their choice.

Are they going to choose life or death?

It is not for the policy-forming process of the capitalist world to answer this question decisively. It has, really speaking, no answer to offer. Or, the only answer that it has—that of a nuclear holocaust—is untenable. It is untenable because of the very nature of the contemporary revolution in science and technology. Therefore, there is no point for the Marxist either to imagine that "capitalism will first be destroyed in a final all-out war, after which there will be a firm basis for world peace." Still, since capitalism is not going to quit the scene voluntarily, there must be a decisive struggle. But this struggle is going to be fought mainly in the soil of the capitalist world, for it can only be the struggle between the working class and the capitalist class. I am afraid that no amount of rethinking on the part of the Marxists or of anybody else is going to alter this basic historical law. It is true, as Somerville says, "the process of replacing capitalism with socialism is one that will be resisted by capitalism with all the weapons at its disposal." Where I fail to agree with him is that such weapons are going to include the most highly developed weapons of physical destruction, that is, nuclear and other such weapons. If the contemporary revolution in science and technology deters the capitalist class from sending these weapons to a distance of several thousand miles, their possible use in the homeland against the working class is too absurd to speak of.

Thus, it is ultimately for the working class—the people—to intervene. But the grave responsibility of the philosophers—or, more broadly, of the intellectuals—cannot be overlooked. A lot of intellectual debris is dumped on the consciousness of the working class—and the mass media are extensively used to anesthetize people in various ways—so that they are prevented from seeing the "evil and destructive system which maims, oppresses and dishonors those who live under it, and which threatens devastation and death to millions of others around the globe."[15] The philosophers, if they do not sell their souls, are primarily expected to remove such debris and thus to enable the working class to see truth. They can best communicate to the people that, although the contemporary revolution in science and technology actually creates the potentials for plenty, an irrational economic and social order wants to make only a hangman of it.

I do not want to overstate the difficulties of the philosophers in the capitalist countries. What I want to add, however, is that I refuse to despair.

NOTES

1. Robert Jungk, *Brighter than a Thousand Suns* (New York: Harcourt Brace, 1958), p. 311-12.

2. See especially P. M. S. Blackett, *Fear, War and the Bomb: Military and Political Consequences of Atomic Energy* (New York: Whittlesey House, 1949); and idem, *Studies of War, Nuclear and Conventional* (New York: Hill and Wang, 1962).

3. Paul A. Baran and Paul M. Sweezy, *Monopoly Capital: An Essay on the American Economic and Social Order* (New York: Monthly Review Press, 1968), p. 191.

4. Ibid., p. 186.

5. Ibid.

6. Ibid., p. 173.

7. Ibid., p. 213.

8. John Desmond Bernal, *Science in History* (London: Pelican, 1969), p. 1152.

9. Ibid., p. 1254.

10. Baran and Sweezy, *Monopoly Capital*, p. 212.
11. Ibid., p. 213.
12. Ibid., p. 212. Reference is to Professor Sumner Slichter.
13. Ibid., p. 211.
14. Ibid., p. 212. Senator Richard B. Russell.
15. Ibid., p. 367.

5
Marxism-Leninism, World Peace, and World Revolution

K. T. FANN (Canada)

It is true that there has been relatively little discussion of the problem of war and peace among academic philosophers. But academic philosophers are typically behind their times. It is not true, however, that there has not been public discussion of this important problem among Marxists. In fact, the question of war and peace was the rock on which the Second International met its doom, and the same question has been a vital issue splitting the world communist movement today.

Ever since capitalism evolved into imperialism, the question of war and peace has been the focal point in the struggle between Marxism-Leninism and revisionism. Before World War I, the leaders of the Second International set out to revise Marxism systematically. The essence of their view on the question of war is that the technical advance in armaments had changed the nature of war qualitatively and that Marxism therefore needed to be revised. Kautsky said, ". . . the next war will not only bring want and misery, but will basically put an end to civilization. . . ."[1] Consequently, the distinction between just and unjust wars is no longer valid. Kautsky also said, ". . . in present-day conditions, there is no such thing as a war which is not a misfortune for nations in general and for the proletariat in particular. What we discussed was the means by which we could prevent a threatening war, and not which wars are useful and which harmful."[2]

Accordingly, Kautsky propagated the theory that weapons decide everything and opposed revolutionary armed struggle. He said, "As has been often stated, one of the reasons why the coming revolutionary struggles will more rarely be fought out by military means lies in the colossal superiority in armaments of the armies of modern states over the arms which are at the disposal of 'civilians' and which usually render any resistance on the part of the latter hopeless from the very outset."[3] According to him, the avoidance of war overshadows all other great world problems, such as capitalism and imperialism. Kautsky said, "The yearning for perpetual peace increasingly inspires the majority of cultured nations. It temporarily pushes the essentially great problem of our times into the background. . . ."[4] From this, revisionism degenerated into bourgeois pacifism. Thus, Bernstein said, "Peace on earth and good will to all men! We should not pause or rest and must attend to the unhindered advance of society towards prosperity in the interests of all, towards equality of rights among nations through international agreement and disarmament."[5]

Lenin correctly pointed out that ". . . the main thing that is usually forgotten on the question of war . . . is that people forget the fundamental question of the class character of the war; why the war broke out; the classes that are waging it; the historical and historico-economic conditions that gave rise to it."[6] Lenin's thesis is that war is inevitable as long as imperialism and the system of exploitation of man by man exist. The possibility of war will disappear only when the division of mankind into classes and all exploitation of man by man and of one nation by another nation are abolished. Until that day arrives, we must study each kind of war separately according to different situations. There are different types of war and different types of peace. There are imperialist wars, national liberation wars, and revolutionary civil wars. Lumping just wars and unjust wars together and opposing all of them is a bourgeois pacifist and not a Marxist approach.

"Socialists cannot, without ceasing to be socialists, be opposed to all war,"[7] said Lenin. Lenin was opposed to imperialist wars but was unconditionally in favor of national wars of liberation and revolutionary civil wars. He said, "To deny all possibility of national wars under imperialism is wrong in theory, obviously mistaken historically, and in practice is tantamount to European chauvinism."[8] It is equally clear that revolutionary civil wars are inevitable when the bourgeois reactionaries suppress the people in their own countries by force of arms. Lenin said, ". . . civil wars are also wars. Whoever recognizes the class struggle cannot fail to recognize civil wars, which in every class society are the natural, and under certain conditions, the inevitable continuation . . . of the class struggle."[9] This is the case because of the simple and fundamental fact that "In every class society, whether it is based on slavery, serfdom, or . . . on wage labor, the oppressing class is armed."[10] There is no way out of a class society except by means of the class struggle—including its most intensive form, armed struggle.

A corollary of Lenin's dictum on war is that socialists cannot, without ceasing to be socialists, be in favor of all peace. We cannot support bourgeois "peace," by which they mean their freedom to exploit and oppress in peace. We are all opposed to bloodshed, violence, and death, but we must say with Lenin, "capitalist society is always an *endless horror,*"[11] and at the same time, we must realize that the birthpangs of a revolution are far less painful than the chronic agony of the old society.

Lenin's thesis on war is summarized thus: "Theoretically, it would be quite wrong to forget that every war is but the continuation of politics by other means; the present imperialist war is the continuation of the imperialist politics of two groups of Great Powers, and these politics were engendered and fostered by the sum total of the relationships of the imperialist epoch. But this very epoch must also necessarily engender and foster the politics of struggle against national oppression and of the proletarian struggle against the bourgeoisie, and therefore, also the possibility and the inevitability, first, of revolutionary national rebellions and wars; second, of proletarian wars and rebellions *against* the bourgeoisie; and, third, of a combination of both kinds of revolutionary war, etc."[12]

History shows that Lenin was right and that the revisionists of the Second International were wrong. Imperialism has succeeded in launching two world wars and has waged numerous wars of other kinds. The world system of exploitation of man by man and oppression of nation by nation has given rise to numerous wars of national liberation and proletarian revolutions as predicted by Lenin. The revisionists' call for disarmament fell on the deaf ears of the imperialists; it only disarmed the fighting spirit of the working-class movement in Europe. In the end, the old revisionists shed their peace masks, sided with their respective imperialist governments when World War I broke out, voted for military appropriations in parliament, and urged the working class of their own countries to plunge into the war and to slaughter their class brothers in other countries. Revisionism in theory was bound to degenerate into reactionary politics in practice.

Is Lenin still right in this age of the technological revolution? Does the technological revolution in weaponry necessitate a revision of Lenin's thesis on war and peace? Is the modern revisionist (or the creative developer of Lenin) justified in revising Lenin's thesis on war and peace?

A cursory comparison of statements of the modern revisionists (such as Khrushchev and some speakers on this colloquium) on the question of war and peace with those of the old revisionists shows an amazing similarity. The heart of the modern revisionists' thesis is that the emergence of nuclear weapons has changed the nature of war. They say, "The nuclear rocket weapons that were created in the middle of our century changed the old conceptions about war."[13] They claim that the appearance of nuclear weapons invalidates the difference between just and unjust wars. They claim that "the atomic bomb does not adhere to the class principle" and that it "does not distinguish between the imperialists and the working people. . . ."[14] They warn against revolutionary wars and wars of national liberation, lest such wars lead to the destruction of mankind. They say, ". . . any small 'local war' might spark off the conflagration of a world war," and "Today, any sort of war, though it may break out as an ordinary non-nuclear war, is likely to develop into a destructive nuclear-missile conflagration." Thus, they say, ". . . the struggle to prevent the nuclear war is the central task facing the anti-imperialist forces in the present epoch" and that it is "the precondition to the solution of all other problems."[15] They spread the illusion that it is possible to bring about a world without weapons, without armed forces, and without wars through general and complete disarmament while the system of the exploitation of man by man still exists.

Like the old revisionists, modern revisionists confuse cause and effect and lump all kinds of wars together. We all wish for a world without weapons; we all want world peace. The only question is how to achieve it. World peace will not be a bit closer no matter how strongly we desire it. Was Lenin wrong when he said, "Only after the proletariat has disarmed the bourgeoisie will it be able, without betraying its world-historical mission, to throw all armaments on the scrap heap; and the proletariat will undoubtedly do this, *but only when this condition has been fulfilled, certainly not before.*"[16]

What are the facts in the modern world? It is obvious that imperialism remains the source of modern wars and that U.S. imperialism is the main force of aggression and war in the contemporary world. Since World War II, U.S. imperialism, stepping into the shoes of the fascists, has been endeavoring to consolidate a vast world empire such as has never been known before. The "global strategy" of U.S. imperialism has been to dominate the intermediate zone lying between the United States and the socialist camp, to put down the revolutions of the oppressed peoples and nations, and to proceed to destroy the socialist countries. This "global strategy" has been responsible for most of the modern wars and international tensions.

The birth of atom bombs certainly has not changed the nature of capitalism or imperialism, nor has it changed the nature of the class struggle and the struggle for national liberation. Has the atom bomb changed the nature of war? That depends on what kind of war you are talking about. Obviously, it has not changed the nature of wars of national liberation or revolutionary civil wars. They have occurred, and some of them directly involved

U.S. imperialism. They have weakened the forces of imperialism and strengthened the forces that prevent the imperialists from using the atom bomb and launching a new world war. Yes, the nature of world war has changed. The horrible destructiveness of nuclear weapons and the fact that the imperialists no longer hold the monopoly of those weapons have so far prevented the imperialists from launching a world war. But we must not confuse the possibility of preventing a new world war with the possibility of preventing all wars. In fact, the imperialists themselves are fully aware that they can no longer rely on their nuclear blackmail to scare the people into submission. They have prepared themselves for "special warfare" and have fought local wars.

When the modern revisionists say that we should change our conceptions and attitudes about war, to whom are they talking? Are they talking to socialists and the oppressed, or are they talking to imperialists and the oppressor? The oppressed peoples and nations have no nuclear weapons, and they cannot use them to make revolutions, nor is it feasible. A socialist country with nuclear weapons certainly cannot support the revolutionary struggles of an oppressed people or nation by nuclear weapons. The sole reason for a socialist country to have nuclear weapons is for defense, for resisting imperialist nuclear threats. No socialists advocate the insane idea that capitalism must "first be destroyed in a final, all-out war, after which there will be a firm basis for world peace." The imperialists are the only ones who need to be preached at; they are the sources of war; they are the threats to world peace.

Some people are so preoccupied with nuclear weapons that they exaggerate the role of technological change. In the view of Marxist-Leninists, people are the makers of history, man is the decisive factor. The Vietnamese people have proved this thesis beyond a shadow of a doubt. The emergence of nuclear weapons can neither arrest the progress of human history nor save the imperialist system from its doom, any more than the emergence of new techniques could save the old systems from their doom in the past. The emergence of nuclear weapons does not and cannot resolve the fundamental contradictions in the contemporary world, does not and cannot alter the law of class struggle, nor does it change the nature of capitalism and imperialism.

It cannot, therefore, be said that with the emergence of nuclear weapons Lenin's thesis on war and peace has become outmoded. There is soil for wars as long as imperialism and the system of exploitation of man by man exist. The destruction of capitalism and imperialism is the precondition for achieving world peace. To prevent a new world war and to defend world peace, there is no other way but for all the oppressed peoples, nations, and peace forces to unite and form the broadest united front against imperialism. No matter how paradoxical this may sound, it reflects the only realistic program: world peace can only be achieved through world revolution.

NOTES

1. Karl Kautsky, *Social-Democracy in War*, cited in *Two Different Lines on the Question of War and Peace* (Peking: Foreign Languages Press, 1963), p. 2.
2. Ibid., p. 3.
3. Ibid., p. 4.
4. Ibid.
5. Bernstein's speech at the Congress of the German Social-Democratic party in Chemnitz, 1912, published in the *Handbook of the Congress of the Social-Democratic Party in 1910-1913*, Vol. 2.
6. V. I. Lenin, *War and Revolution, Collected Works*, 4th Russian ed. (Moscow: SPHPL, 1949), 24: 362.
7. *Lenin on War and Peace* (Peking: Foreign Languages Press, 1970), p. 59.
8. Ibid., p. 60.
9. Ibid.
10. Ibid., p. 63.
11. Ibid.
12. Ibid., p. 62.
13. *The Open Letter of the Central Committee of the CPSU* (Moscow: Foreign Languages Press, 1963).
14. Ibid.
15. Ibid.
16. *Lenin on War and Peace*, p. 63.

6
Why Socialism Needs Peace
ERWIN HERLITZIUS (GDR)

In our discussion of "Technology, Peace, and Contemporary Marxism," I want, above all, to advocate the coercive demand "that all states that possess nuclear weapons should come to an agreement that such weapons must not be used, that they must be destroyed, and that no more of them are to be produced," as John Somerville put it.[1]

Indeed, this view of future political life corresponds exactly with the peace program of the community of socialist states, and is expressed in the active policy of peaceful coexistence of states with differing social systems. As everybody knows, the Soviet Union has submitted concrete proposals to this end. Some important steps forward were made, and with a comprehensive system of treaties, we are now (1973) getting closer to a genuine relaxation of tensions in Europe and in the whole world. Consequently, we are following the conception of peaceful coexistence as it is outlined in the continuation of Marxist-Leninist policy since Lenin's worldwide message on peace in 1917.[2] There is indeed "a new theory and practice of morals and politics to go with this new power, in order to continue to survive and progress."[3]

However, the impression given by Somerville is that "all the old habits, practices, and principles" of Marx's theory about war have to be revised or even rejected in accordance with the preventive measures of the Soviet government on account of the so-called Cuban missile crisis of 1962. The "old principles" would have indicated to the Soviet Union, Somerville asserts, not to remove its missiles from Cuba unless the Americans agreed to remove theirs simultaneously from Turkey.

As far as this claim for a wholly new theory is concerned with special regard to the Cuban situation of 1962, the answer must be given as follows: There is a profound, creatively developed heritage of theory and practice in the domain of revolutionary strategy since Marx, Engels, and Lenin. In particular, we refer to the Marxist-Leninist theory on compromises in politics[4] within the theory of strategy and tactics of class struggle. Lenin, more than once and mostly referring to Marx and Engels, has explained that it is impossible to renounce compromises but that, by all means and throughout a compromise, the revolutionary task and the revolutionary interest of the working people are to be maintained and forwarded. This field is wide enough to enclose all organizational tactics of the working class as well as the manifold aspects of class alliance and of the policy of peaceful coexistence among states with differing social systems. But the policy of peaceful coexistence could not be worked out until a socialist state had been founded, and it has been further developed since the union of socialist states has been strong enough in its just struggle to contribute to new possibilities for the progressive forces in the whole world.

We were advised to attach much importance to the pathetic Kennedy story about the Cuban situation of 1962. But these dramatic events once taken into account, why not proceed from them, as effect, to their cause? Let us consider the following quotation from Richard D. Heffner's *A Documentary History of the United States*:

> It was, of course, in the realm of world affairs that the short-lived Kennedy Administration made its most obvious contributions—despite the early Bay of Pigs fiasco, which the new President blundered into halfheartedly endorsing a plan, launched during the previous Administration, to support an abortive attempt by Cuban refugees to "invade" Cuba and to overthrow Communist dictator Fidel Castro.[5]

The author grants that *this was a mistake* and expresses the hope that no such mistake should be made again. In this context, all further activities demonstrate the learning process in the historical worldwide turning to the succeeding policy of peaceful coexistence. A learning process always depends on two sides! It was a helpful stop signal given in 1962 from the Soviet side to leave Cuba untouched. It was an urgent assistance toward developing peace policy. With reasoning from experience, it became obvious that the achievements of socialism in the world are irreversible. Meanwhile, this maxim is to be acknowledged likewise in Europe and in Asia.

If we suppose that someone could have asked Marx or Engels what to do in our situation concerning the use of weapons capable, in their technological development, of eliminating all forms of life from this planet—it seems to me that a Marxist answer never goes from mere technology to politics, but from reasoning about the politics and economy of the one side to the politics and economy of the other side. I suppose that Marx at present would point out that the discovery of the law of uneven socio-economic development of differing capitalist monopolies and states had already been formulated in the first volume of his *Capital* and that with the possibility of socialism being set up not at once in a global unity, but in single countries one by one, then the more attention we give to the class character of anticommunist reactions, the more we would see that the forces of science, technology, and production could be turned into forces of total destructiveness.[6]

To end the Cold War period was and still is primarily not a question of a new technological challenge. To come to agreements on all points concerning the safeguarding of peace on our continent and in the whole world is something the socialist countries, on the basis of their Marxist-Leninist theory, are well prepared to do. The conception of a just war neither was nor is in any contradiction to the interest of the working people. And to invert the relation of cause and effect, the theorems concerning just and unjust wars have a further importance, irrespective of special kinds of weapons. That is, these theorems imply the unveiling of any secrets in which war is born. From this point of view there is all the more reason for unveiling covert activities carried out by the Carter administration since 1978, activities that tended to shift the military equilibrium.

The main interest is and always was to prevent war because the Marxist position is that war involves the killing and injuring of human beings as well as the destruction of material goods.[7] But to eliminate wars from politics depends on the potency of all peace forces in the world, depends on the internationalism of the working class to transform what is historically possible into the most effective power, depends above all on the strength of socialism: the stronger socialism is, the stronger is the community of socialist states and the more secure is peace.

However, to qualify a particular war in history as justifiable is a highly complicated problem. If we say that a war is justified when it represents an act of collective self-defense, or in other words, when force and violence are used against people in violation of their human rights, such people should have the right to use force and violence in return[8]—this could only be a first approach. If a simplified misreading of this sentence in the sense of anarchy or individual terrorism could be excluded on principle, we have to learn even from "classical Marxism" that the working class by its international association never was led to unhesitatingly participate in any kind of so-called collective self-defense in case of an unavoidable war.

Let us consider the problem of drawing distinctions by focusing on the wars of 1870 and 1914. We know how the events of the Franco-Prussian War of 1870-71 had to pass through three stages to reach their climax: First, the decision of A. Bebel and W. Liebknecht in the Norddeutscher Reichstag on July 21, when the vote on the war loan was taken. Their abstention from voting had to take into account not only that the French declaration of war in fact was aimed against the desired unity of the German nation—and in that sense, it was a just war from the German side—but also that Bismarck's policy of "blood and steel" had provoked this calamity. The fact that the predominant interests of the French and German workers were contrary to the overall policy of Prussian chauvinism as experienced in wars like those of 1864 and 1866 made Bebel and Liebknecht stress the dimension of the real danger.⁹ Marx and Engels appreciated this abstention very much despite the fact that this war in its beginning formally was a just war.

The second stage is marked by Bebel's and Liebknecht's voting "no" against a further war-bond issue after the defeat of the French troops in the battle of Sedan and since the proclamation of the French Republic abolished the monarchy, on September 4. And the third stage, as we know, is the partisanship for and solidarity with the proletariat of Paris, when its heroic struggle for the first time in history rose to a short-lived germination of a new type of power, of a proletarian state. In his letter to Kugelmann, Marx stated: "Wie aber der Krieg immer ende, er hat das französische Proletariat in den Waffen geübt, und das ist die beste Garantie der Zukunft."¹⁰ That is, "Whatever the result of this war will be, it has given military experience to the French proletariat"—or, more exactly, "it has enabled the proletariat to take up and use arms, and this is the best guarantee for the future."

To judge the character of World War I, Lenin demanded that the policy preceding the war and all its circumstances must be taken into account and that the interest of the working class is the determining factor.¹¹ Thus, the opportunist slogan "defense of the fatherland" was stigmatized and the imperialist war defined as unjust on both sides.¹² Despite the existence of the most aggressive German imperialism, the other imperialist states had the same interests of expansion. Then the chain of imperialism was broken at its weakest link. It was not by mere accident that the first successful socialist revolution originated in opposition to war. And the stronger socialism is, the less the revolutionary process in the world will be affected by war or could be linked with any kind of war by reactionary forces.

Please let me remark on Somerville's interpretation of Marx's theory on the significance of the "mode of production in material life [that] determines the general character of the social, political and spiritual processes of life."¹³ This quotation presents an insufficient extract from Marx's *Contribution to the Critique of Political Economy* as an easy-to-read version. It seems to be a token of support for the hypothesis that it represents "the historical thesis central to Marx's whole view of society—that qualitative changes . . . at the technological base . . . demand corresponding changes at superstructural levels. . . ."[14]

There is, indeed, an interdependence and interaction between what Marx calls the productive forces (which include all technological driving forces applied in human labor) and the superstructural levels. But there is no immediate influence going from the "technological base" directly to the superstructural levels, such as moral or political principles. This very discovery is central to Marx's whole view of society—that there are basic relations of production or, "what is but a legal expression for the same thing," property relations, which, as the heart of the economic foundation, really create the class character of the ideological content of all superstructural perceptions and institutions. Therefore, permit me to complete that quotation from Marx's *Contribution to the Critique of Political Economy* just with the following axioms:

> In the social production which men carry on they enter into definite relations that are indispensable and independent of their will; these relations of production correspond to a definite stage of development of their material powers of production. The sum total of these relations of production constitutes the economic structure of society—the real foundation, on which rise legal and political superstructures and to which correspond definite forms of social consciousness. . . . It is not the consciousness of men that determines their existence, but, on the contrary, their social existence determines their consciousness.
>
> At a certain stage of their development the material forces of production in society come into conflict with the existing relations of production, or—what is but a legal expression for the same thing— with the property relations within which they had been at work before. From forms of development of the forces of production these relations turn into their fetters. Then comes the period of social revolution. With the change of the economic foundation the entire immense superstructure is more or less rapidly transformed.[15]

The socialist revolution opens up the new era of harmonizing the exigencies of the most productive use of science and technology with the process of developing real humanism. Following this generalization, weapons of total destructiveness can be neither enlisted under the category of productive forces nor identified with any kind of productive modern technology as applied to creative human labor. The category of "property relations" is the apt expression that marks the key position of that class minority on the one side that maintains a technology within a military-industrial complex in order to multiply capitalist profit and power, and, on the other side, of that majority of working people that is in possession of the main means of production in order to link the scientific and technological revolution increasingly with the advantages of the developed socialist society. When a wholly new superstructure has been built on the base of socialist property, when a socialist state has been created with democratic and cultural goals never before known in history, the first of all steps and measures toward reaching the necessary higher quality in the work of peaceful planning and management is the acquisition of Marxist-Leninist knowledge.

By satisfying its developing material and cultural needs, humankind creates itself. Only when comprehensive and far-reaching conscience leads people's minds and determines their actions is there a foundation for a full unfolding of their creative activity in the cause of the all-around strengthening of socialism. At the Technical University of Dresden, I have for many years been working with hundreds of scientists and technicians of all disciplines. Our mutual academic research and teaching have proved to us that a scientific Weltanschauung and new values and moral norms neither spontaneously grow out of technology nor out of problems of controlling weapons capable of eliminating all forms of life from our planet. We learned our lesson of history hard enough to know that it depends on the policy and the class interest, whether or not the means of modern technology serve human beings. And our socialist policy of peaceful coexistence and proletarian internationalism has its root in the socialist relations of production, in the principle of labor, as Marx has put it.[16] Meanwhile, we are going to continue our studies of classical Marxism, too, because, for instance, Marx's final chapter in *Capital* (1867) on the "Historical Tendency of Capitalist Accumulation"[17] demonstrates how "modern" is Marx's prediction of the way from capitalism to socialism. Combined with the further developed Marxism of Lenin and with the rich experience of the working class in its worldwide struggles, our up-to-date theory on war and peace needs nothing but being realized. And never before was the axiom of Marxism of such importance: that the behavior in foreign relations always depends on the way to get along with the real needs of the working people at home.

NOTES

1. John Somerville, "Soviet Marxism and Nuclear War," in *Soviet Marxism and Nuclear War: An International Debate*, ed. John Somerville (Westport, Conn.: Greenwood Press, 1981).
2. V. I. Lenin, *Werke* (Berlin: Dietz Verlag, 1961), Vol. 26, pp. 239 and 346-47 (the decree on peace and the first draft of a program to negotiate a peace).
3. Somerville, "Soviet Marxism and Nuclear War."
4. Lenin, *Werke*, Vol. 5, pp. 370-72, 542-43; Vol. 7, p. 373; Vol. 12, pp. 209, 230-31; Vol. 13, pp. 9-10, 19; Vol. 16, pp. 221-25; Vol. 19, pp. 237-38; Vol. 25, pp. 313-19 (here explicitly referring to Engels' opposition to Blanqui, 1873, Lenin explains that it is impossible to renounce compromises but that by all means throughout a compromise the revolutionary task and the interest of the working people are to be maintained and forwarded); Vol. 26, pp. 6-7, 31-32, 40; Vol. 27, pp. 19-22, 68-69, 246-47, 307-08, 337; Vol. 28, p. 52-55 (Lenin's letter to the American workers about an "agreement" with German imperialism); Vol. 30, pp. 348-49, 484-86 ("About Compromises," March 1920); Vol. 31, pp. 19-24, 52-63 (referring to Engels, a further contribution on principle: "No Compromises at All?"), 67-76, 82, 97-98, 154, 187, 222; Vol. 32, pp. 157-58, 350-52 (referring to Marx about cooperation with capitalists); Vol. 33, p. 204; Vol. 35, p. 69.
5. Richard D. Heffner, *A Documentary History of the United States* (New York: New American Library, 1965), p. 318.
6. Lenin, *Werke*, Vol. 24, p. 401. In the remarkable lecture on "War and Revolution," Lenin analyzes the development of modern technology in relation to the development of capitalist monopolies: they neces-

sarily create this new kind of world war that Engels in 1887 already predicted with an astonishing insight into the effects of the objective economic laws. Engels predicted that 8 to 10 million soldiers would be killed and that the "system of excelling one another with war equipment" could have no consequences but the triumph of the proletariat. See F. Engels's Introduction to Borkheim's *Zur Erinnerung für die deutschen Mordspatrioten*, in Marx/Engels, *Werke*, Vol. 21, pp. 349-51.

7. Somerville, "Soviet Marxism and Nuclear War."
8. Ibid.
9. K. Marx, "The General Council of the International Workingmen's Association on the War (July 23, 1870)," in Marx/Engels, *Werke*, Vol. 17, pp. 2-7. Referring to the address of 1864, this draft starts by asking: "If the emancipation of the working classes requires their fraternal concurrence, how are they to fulfill that great mission with a foreign policy in pursuit of criminal designs, playing upon national prejudices and squandering in piratical wars the people's blood and treasure?"
10. Marx/Engels, *Werke*, Vol. 33, p. 164.
11. Lenin, *Werke*, Vol. 23, p. 23.
12. Ibid., Vol. 24, pp. 395-420.
13. Somerville, "Soviet Marxism and Nuclear War."
14. Ibid.
15. K. Marx, *A Contribution to the Critique of Political Economy*. Excerpt in Marx and Engels, *Basic Writings*, ed. L. S. Feuer (New York: Doubleday, 1959), pp. 43-44.
16. Somerville, "Soviet Marxism and Nuclear War." "Marx's First Address of the General Council of the International Workingmen's Association on the War" (July 23, 1870) concludes with the following proclamation: "Die englische Arbeiterklasse reicht den französischen wie den deutschen Arbeitern brüderlich die Hand. Sie ist fest überzeugt, das . . . die Allianz der Arbeiter aller Länder schliesslich die Kriege ausrotten wird . . . Diese einzige grosse Tatsache, ohnegleichen in der Geschichte der Vergangenheit, eroffnet die Aussicht auf eine hellere Zukunft. Sie beweist, das: im Gegensatz zur alten Gesellschaft mit ihrem ökonomischen Elend und ihrem politischen Wahnwitz, eine neue Gesellschaft entsteht, deren internationales Prinzip der Friede sein wird, weil bei jeder Nation dasselbe Prinzip herrscht—die Arbeit!" ["The English working class stretches the hand of fellowship to the French and German working people. They feel deeply convinced that whatever turn the impending regrettable war may take, the alliance of the working classes of all countries will ultimately put an end to war.

The very fact that while official France and Germany are rushing into fratricidal strife, the workmen of France and Germany send each other messages of peace and goodwill: this great fact, unparalleled in the history of the past, opens the vista of a brighter future. It proves that in contrast to the old society, with its economic miseries and its political delirium, a new society is springing up, whose international rule will be Peace, because its national ruler will be everywhere the same—Labor!"]

17. Feuer, ed., *Basic Writings*, pp. 164-67.

7

Marxism, Technological Development, and World Peace

ADAM SCHAFF (Poland)

Let me begin with a short remark that I have already made to my friend John Somerville. After his brilliant paper, I am in a very embarrassing position. First, it was a remarkable paper given by one of the best prepared people in the world to talk on the problems of peace and war. I am not one of those people. But he invited me to present a paper on any aspect of the theme, and in my brief report, I am going to draw your attention to a different dimension of the problem. This procedure follows the guidelines of the organizers of this colloquium, the American Society for the Philosophical Study of Marxism.

What I wish to do is to cope with some problems linked to the title of our colloquium, Technology, Peace, and Contemporary Marxism, showing the impact upon them of the development of modern technology, putting all this into the framework of war and peace at the end.

When we raise the problem of technology in relation to contemporary Marxism, we mean by it the *development* of technology in our day and its impact on the *problématique* of contemporary Marxism. It is a right and a very "orthodox" way of raising this problem to do so in the context of the relations between the so-called base and the superstructure. While the influence of the base is primary, it is understood in the light of Marxism that there also exists a specific feedback in the form of a reciprocal impact of the superstructure on the base. However, at this point, we wish to dwell on the first element of this complicated correlation. I will do this, trying to underline in the first place the problems that have arisen in this situation to confront Marxist thinking, conditioning its further development.

Having in mind the rapid development of modern technology, we often label it—and rightly so—as a scientific-technological revolution. In doing this, we do not always—especially on the highly abstract level of philosophical thinking—fully realize at least two factors that should play a dominant role in our deliberations today. These factors are: first, that we are already now going through this revolution, and that we must therefore have a concrete picture of its further development if we wish to understand its possible consequences; and second, what these consequences are, the germ of which can be seen already today, and whose blossoms and fruit must be expected in the near future, for which we must prepare now.

The word "revolution," connected with technological development, rightly stresses the point that what is meant is not simply quantitative change in the old technology, but changes of quality, changes of the paradigm, as modern theoreticians of scientific development would phrase it. This "revolution" consists, among other things, in the following three, organically interconnected new scientific phenomena: cybernetics, computer techniques, and automation. It is not our task here, nor would we have the time for it, to enter into the details of the essential novelty of these scientific discoveries and of the character of their interconnections and mutual conditioning. It is enough to say here that this trio interests us as a specific unity, taking into account the social consequences of these new developments.

Let us now—as was mentioned above—indicate some of the developments that are of special importance. It is understood that we are making a conscious selection of some items among many; we are choosing those that raise problems to be analyzed and solved by Marxism in a new way.

Let us begin with automation. This new development in technology, which will be applied to the entire process of production in the countries of high industrial development during the next twenty or thirty years, implies revolutionary changes not only from the point of view of the technology of production but also from the point of view of the social life of humanity. This perspective raises a plentitude of problems: economic, political, and social, all of them of great importance. Out of these, I select one, which looks very modest but which penetrates into the very depths of each society—whatever its economic, political, and social order—and which demands immediate attention. I have in mind a phenomenon that I label "the pollution of free time."

The inevitability of automation, including full automation, already was foreseen in a brilliant way by Marx in the middle of the nineteenth century, when he described this development in the first draft of *Das Kapital* in 1857 (then titled *Grundrisse*). Analyzing the consequences of this process, he said three things that would have amazed many Marxists before the publication of this manuscript with its enormous value for the comprehension of Marx and his thought: that the work of the human being will cease to play the main role in the process of production,[1] that a dominant role will then be played by science, and that science as a means of production becomes a part of the base.[2] For subsequent Marxists, the phenomenon of automation thus became—in any case theoretically—nothing surprising in itself. But facing the practical, social consequences of automation, a Marxist must remember also another thesis of Marx, which runs like a red thread through his works from the Paris manuscripts of his youth, through the Grundrisse, and on to the last volume of *Das Kapital*: that the *real* life of the human being begins with leisure, that is, when the person stops "working," and this—as Marx stresses in *Das Kapital*—holds for all economic formations.

However, at the present time, we risk facing a situation wherein the abundance of leisure, which will come with the development of full automation capable of reducing human "work" to a minimum hardly imaginable today, may lead to the "pollution" of leisure. That is, humans who are not prepared for a life without work in the traditional sense of the word may suffer all kinds of disturbances just because they have too much free time, which they are not prepared to consume. Let us add immediately that this is not a utopian futurology but is something imminent:

the perspective of twenty or thirty years is a very short one in which to handle such problems. Moreover, even a short-term program, for example, to handle the problem of a third free day in a week, not to mention a fourth, creates a difficult and urgently practical issue.

Has Marxism a basis and a possibility to find solutions to such problems? Yes, it has. Not in a form of already-given answers—Marxism is not a prophecy; it is a scientific theory—but in the form of basic theses, which can and should be further developed. The problem we are raising is in reality a sort of syndrome, a complex of many interconnected problems. Let us define some of them, without however entering into the core of their solution, which would require more time than we have on this occasion.

We know that Marx took over from the utopian Socialists—from Saint-Simon and Fourier—two postulates that are of fundamental importance for the comprehension of Marx's socialism: (1) society must overcome the antagonism between labor in the cities and labor on the land and (2) it must overcome the antagonism between physical labor and intellectual labor. It was quite clear from the beginning that both these postulates were aiming at the realization of the central postulate of Marx's socialism: the development of a new type of person, a universal person, as Marx phrased it. But at the same time, there was the feeling that these postulates were utopian because no realistic way of their implementation in practical life could be indicated. However, with the computerization and automation of modern society, we are achieving a situation where these postulates are becoming—in highly industrialized countries—fully realistic. A heap of new problems, sometimes old ones but lost from our attention on the difficult paths of constructing the everyday life of socialist countries, arises in connection with this: how to plan the new living centers of human beings, how to handle the new working population that becomes more and more a direct agent of science, and, most important, how to develop and implement Marx's model of the universal person.

Here we come to grips with our main problem: the "pollution" of free time.

Modern psychiatry, especially the school of logotherapy, has shown empirically that persons in modern societies, because of all kinds of social and psychological conditions, suffer from mental disturbances that can, in a very general way, be reduced to the so-called existential vacuum. Philosophically speaking, when a person loses the "sense of life," this loss can become the basis of mental disturbances, not only in terms of a given individual but also as a phenomenon of social insanity. Such a loss becomes, to a large extent, the cause of negative phenomena among the younger generation in the so-called consumer societies. We can foresee, on the basis of these and similar experiences, many problems for persons "freed from the curse of Jehovah," that is, from work in the traditional sense of the word, which was an important element of their "sense of life," one that must be replaced by something better. To say it simply: human beings must have their lives filled with clear-cut aims and obligations to find their "sense of life" and in order not to become victims of all kinds of "escapes" from the annoying void that is created when one has what one needs to live, but does not know what to live for. An exception here is the creative intellectuals, who in the changed situation do not change their way of working—whether as scientists, writers, painters, composers, or the like. But even with a large increase in their number in the future society, they will remain nevertheless a minority. And what about the rest, that is, the huge majority of the population?

Just here steps in the Marxian postulate and model of the universal person. Why not expand the traditional concept of work, which will to a large extent disappear, into a new, a wider one? Why not make out of the whole society a learning or creative society, thus giving to people new aims and obligations and filling the gap caused by the loss of their "sense of life"? This is a way, however complex, of implementing Marx's postulate concerning the development of a new, universal person.

Of course, this general thesis must be concretized. I have done this elsewhere, but in its general form, it shows one of the possible ways out of a difficult situation. It shows it on the basis of Marxist thought, and it shows it as a program for elaborating problems that are becoming imminent while there is relatively little time left to find a solution for them.

And how are these problems related to peace? In a most direct way: peace is a *conditio sine qua non* not only for the very development of the phenomena we were talking about but also for finding solutions to problems raised by them. We are living in an epoch when the saying, "all ways are now leading to socialism" becomes in the perspective of full automation ever more confirmed. This inevitable development toward socialism in this or that form, bringing a solution to the problems posed to humanity by the scientific-technological revolution, can be endangered by war because, under the conditions of contemporary technology, war could mean annihilation of humanity and thus the end of its development. Therefore, the pseudorevolutionary phraseology of all kinds of "leftists," directed against the policy of peaceful coexistence, not only is nonsense but also includes a threat to humanity. The battle for peace must be continued, and in today's conditions, it has a revolutionary content: it contains the guarantee of continuation of a social development that yields at least the possibility of finding solutions to the impending problems brought into the world by modern technology.

NOTES

1. Karl Marx, *Grundrisse* (Berlin: Dietz Verlag, 1953), p. 592. This work, the first draft of *Das Kapital*, was first published in the Soviet Union in 1939, but, as the entire Soviet edition was destroyed in the war, the Dietz edition, which replaced it, is regarded as the first. Translations into languages other than German began in 1967. The first in English was the Penguin edition of 1970. The work contains not only Marx's economic views, but many extremely important philosophical and sociological comments. Any serious study of Marx today must take it into account.

2. Ibid., p. 594.

8
Are the Theses of Classical Marxism on Just War and Violence Valid Today?
ADOLFO SÁNCHEZ VÁSQUEZ (Mexico)

I would like to respond to the question posed by John Somerville in this colloquium: Do the technological changes that have been produced since Marx and Engels—and in consequence the changes produced in the means of destruction—oblige us to revise the theses of classical Marxism on just war and violence? Does a just war become unjust when the side defending itself uses weapons that threaten the very existence of the human race?

It is clear that this applies to a socialist country only as a matter of self-defense, since a socialist country will never launch a war of aggression; moreover, among socialist countries, it applies only to one that is an atomic power, like the Soviet Union and perhaps, or soon, China. But even though the question narrows itself down in this way, we find, along with the posing of it, a proposed reply that seems clear: we must renounce our cause, that is, the just war, in order to uphold a supreme cause, the survival of the human race.

We take into account that our discussion concerns a theoretical problem or a possibility of the future. However, Somerville reminds us that there is already a historical precedent: the October missile crisis in Cuba. More exactly, there is already a historical example of this renunciation of our cause in order to ensure the survival of the human race as the supreme cause.

If one considers this thesis of the unjustifiability of the just war in the epoch of the technological revolution, I think it becomes necessary to approach the question from the side of our conception of history and society. From the philosophical point of view—for us the philosophy of Marxism—it is necessary to take account of the decisive importance of the productive forces, of technology and material production.

But we cannot forget another thesis of classical Marxism: "History is made by human beings." To be sure, not by human beings in general, or taken in abstraction, but real persons as they live together in groups and relate to one another in terms of their membership in different classes. As Marx and Engels say in the *Communist Manifesto*: "The class struggle is the motive force of history."

However, if the class struggle is the motive force of history, the force that brings about the major historical and social changes, and among these, in the first place, brings about revolutions, is it possible that in our time the technological revolution rather than the class struggle is the decisive factor? If we agree with the saying that Lenin borrowed from Clausewitz, that "war is the continuation of politics by other means," then war, foreign or domestic, is the continuation of the class struggle by other means. But in that case, under the conditions of the technological revolution and the new means of destruction, how could we carry on the class struggle and just wars as a continuation of that struggle? Is it then necessary to forget the thesis that the class struggle is the motive force, the decisive factor of history, and to consider that the productive forces, the scientific and technological revolution, play the dominant role?

Classical Marxism, including Lenin, says that human beings and their concrete forms of action (that is to say, the struggle of classes) are the decisive factor, not the degree of scientific and technological development. But let us look to the concrete problem before us, the problem of the use and justification of war in the epoch of the technological revolution. Now if we accept the suggested renunciation—and above all if imperialism is aware that the socialist countries and in general the peoples of the whole world accept this renunciation of the just war in face of the menace of an atomic catastrophe—such renunciation will be able to avert or avoid an atomic war, but this will not lead to a true peace.

How can we reach a true peace while the very nature of imperialism is war, aggression, and intervention? The answer lies in the fact that imperialism does not like to commit suicide, and for that reason does not want a general atomic war; but it cannot renounce conventional wars, aggression, or permanent intervention.

Look at the whole history of Latin America up to now, 1973: yesterday, Mexico; today, Santo Domingo, Cuba, and—why not —the Chile of Allende. Imperialism does not and cannot prefer general atomic war, but it also does not prefer true peace. What, then, does it prefer, and above all, what does it do? It makes conventional war against countries like Vietnam, and it carries on atomic blackmail since it cannot make atomic war (the examples are clear in the case of the Cuban missile crisis and throughout the Vietnam war).

We know that the revolutionary government and people of Cuba did not accept the atomic blackmail during the Cuban missile crisis, and that the government and people of Vietnam did not accept the blackmail in their case. Thus, we do not have atomic war, and we do not have true peace. We have, on one side, aggression, intervention, conventional war, and atomic blackmail; on the other side, we have the struggle of oppressed peoples, which sometimes takes the form of popular wars, naturally just wars.

In that case, what is the true nature of the struggle for peace and peaceful coexistence? This question is inseparable from the problem raised at the outset. It is necessary to understand that peaceful coexistence between great powers is vital to all the people of the world. In peaceful coexistence there is common ground for capitalist powers and socialist countries to avoid atomic war.

But the concrete content of this coexistence cannot consist in that which gives it its vital importance. For imperialism, this coexistence means not only a guarantee of peace with the socialist atomic powers but also the possibility of continuing, without the risk of nuclear war, its aggression, intervention, and conventional warfare against selected peoples. For socialism, this coexistence operates to create the most favorable conditions, in the existing circumstances, for the construction of a new society and also for giving help to other peoples as part of the same world revolutionary process.

If the coexistence operates to restrain or limit this struggle for a new society, then it will only serve imperialism, and will contribute neither to the struggle of other peoples nor to socialism itself. All that has happened in this most recent period has confirmed the fact that imperialism, in preferring to avoid atomic war, considers peaceful coexistence to be compatible with aggression, intervention, and conventional war.

This is why it is necessary to say once again—and not at all by way of an argument from authority—that the thesis of classical Marxism to the effect that as long as capitalism exists as a world system there will be wars (not necessarily atomic wars, but conventional wars) is a valid thesis.

There is only one possibility of true peace and of the abolition of all forms of war (atomic, conventional, civil): the destruction of capitalism and the construction of a new, socialist society in its place. Because of this, the problem of true peace is inseparable from the problem of socialism. Thus, socialism is today more necessary than ever, more necessary than in the time of Marx because, in the epoch of the technological revolution, socialism is necessary not only to ensure the development of humanity but also to guarantee the survival of the human race.

However, in the transition from capitalism to socialism, the problem of the role of violence once again arises, and once again it is necessary to ask whether or not the theory of classical Marxism on violence is valid. Everyone knows what this thesis is: in class society, violence is a historical necessity. We may add that in a world where violence dominates, peaceful, nonviolent means cannot radically transform society. Nonviolence cannot abolish violence. In *State and Revolution*, Lenin said: "In general the bourgeois state cannot be replaced by the proletarian state without using violent means."

Marx always emphasized the role of violence in history. However, it also is true that he accepted the possibility of a peaceful transition to socialism, although only under exceptional conditions. That is, when revolutionary violence occurs, it is in response to the violence of a state with a strong military apparatus. Only in a bourgeois democratic country where the proletariat obtains a parliamentary majority and where the military-bureaucratic apparatus is weak, is there the possibility of a peaceful transition. In his polemic with Kautsky, Lenin interpreted Marx in this sense. All historical experience past and present confirms this thesis of classical Marxism on the determining—not the exclusive—role of violence.

The most recent hope of a peaceful transition to socialism was in Chile, where the reactionary forces that had for three years used against the democratic, peaceful, and legal government of Chile all sorts of violent and illegal means (sabotage, terrorist attacks, assassinations), finally employed the most violent and illegal means of all: military sedition supported by yankee imperialism. It is clear that President Allende and his party had the government but not the power. His party did not by itself have a parliamentary majority, nor could it count on the bureaucratic-military apparatus (the army), the two conditions that Marx had emphasized.

Thus, we see that in regard to the role of violence within a country, as well as in regard to its role in the external relations between countries, in the form of war, the thesis of classical Marxism continues to be valid, although the new conditions oblige us in each concrete situation to apply it in a way that takes account of the actual, concrete conditions.

9
Psychology, Morality, and Nuclear Holocaust
RONALD HIRSCHBEIN (USA)

> We condemn to death without emotion
> and there is no singular personal death to be had
> only an anonymous cheapened death
> which we could dole out to entire nations
> on a mathematical basis.
> (Declaration of the Marquis de Sade
> in Peter Weiss's *Marat/Sade*.)

As social critic Paul Goodman observed, modern warfare has become much less angry but much more destructive. To begin to cope with this irony, three questions are addressed in this paper: What is the nature of contemporary international violence? What state of consciousness produces it? What might be done to alter this state of consciousness?

Many Americans—and all too many other people—witness, condone, and commit international atrocities with little apparent emotional involvement or moral responsibility. Examples of this behavior, which I call the Adolf Eichmann syndrome, are numerous. For instance, the American public seemed more outraged by rising meat prices than by the rising death toll from American bombs in Indochina. And Lieutenant Calley erred, not

Author's Note: I wish to express special thanks for the critique of my work offered by my friend and former colleague Dr. Ross Gandy of Cuernavaca.

because he murdered, but because he became personally involved with his Song My victims; no scandal would have occurred had he murdered unemotionally from invisible airplanes —as thousands of his comrades had done.

This syndrome is a new mode of aggression in which the belligerent subject is detached from violence: he merely follows orders coordinating or triggering the death-dealing technology of warfare. In fact, technological terror has become so common and standardized that even the most heinous acts have become banal, as Herbert Marcuse recognizes:

> These new modes of aggression destroy without getting one's hands dirty, one's body soiled, one's mind incriminated. The killer remains clean, physically as well as mentally. The purity of his deadly work obtains added sanction if it is directed against the national enemy in the national interest.[1]

Adolf Eichmann is alive and well inside many of the people in our culture: How is this possible?

This syndrome should be understood not as an isolated modern aberration but as the outcome of certain historically mediated mental processes—in short, a world view. Now world views do not exist abstractly; they exist in history and are applied in ways that usually reproduce and extend the dominion of the ruling class. But where are we to turn to find a detailed and systematic articulation of the world view that generates the syndrome under discussion?

Marx might answer that philosophers often unwittingly tend to reflect and legitimize the world view essential to the emerging ruling class. Philosophic systems might be considered harbingers of what is destined to occur in popular consciousness; indeed, philosophy is sometimes the common sense of subsequent centuries. At the close of the eighteenth century, Immanuel Kant crystallized the most cherished and unquestioned assumptions of a future culture. With this in mind, we turn to the thinker often called the greatest modern philosopher, Immanuel Kant, not forgetting what Engels once said:

The German bourgeois-philistine runs through German philosophy from Kant to Hegel, sometimes positively and sometimes negatively.[2]

Kant provides the best insight into the ideology that generates the Adolf Eichmann syndrome because he delineates its essential preconditions in his epistemology and ethics. While it certainly was not the purpose of the author of *Perpetual Peace* to provide the underpinnings for passionless modern atrocities, it was nevertheless his historical function to reflect, articulate, and legitimize a world view that is the sine qua non of advanced capitalism and some of its most pernicious ideology.

This world view, a popularized version of Newtonian mechanics, defines all phenomenal reality as machines (ultimately, matter in motion) operating in Newtonian space and time.[3] Prior to Kant, this mechanical world view was merely instrumental in the domination of nature, but Kant's philosophy reveals the power of machine-mindedness to dominate consciousness itself. As Marcuse observes:

> The principles of modern science were *a priori* structured in such a way that they could serve as conceptual instruments for a universe of self-propelling, productive control. . . . The scientific method which led to the ever-more-effective domination of nature thus came to provide the pure concepts . . . for the ever-more-effective domination of man by man through the domination of nature.[4]

Kant's philosophy is the very embodiment of these "pure concepts," for in one of the boldest reifications in all philosophy he argued that consciousness itself must inevitably impose the mechanical world view on all possible experience. Prior to Kant, only the external world was reduced to mechanisms; with the advent of Kant, consciousness itself was reduced to predictable operations. Philosopher of science E. A. Burtt recognized the consequences of the Newtonian world view when he wrote:

> Now the world is an infinite and monotonous mathematical machine. Not only is his [man's] high place in a cosmic telelogy lost, but all these things which were the very substance of the physical world to the scholastic—the things that made it alive and lovely and spiritual

—are lumped ... into the human nervous and circulatory systems. ...
It was simply an incalculable change in the viewpoint of the world
held by intelligent opinion in Europe.[5]

There were economic reasons why Kant reified ideas whose time had come. The exploits of capitalism required what Weber called a new rationality: an entire society consistently organized for the sake of corporate profit. This capitalist rationality reproduces itself through the creation of the rational (i.e., consistent) individual so systematically portrayed by Kant. In his epistemology, consciousness becomes as totally standardized as the most efficient assembly line: all possible experience is packaged in the Newtonian world view. And in his ethics, consistency is elevated to the *summum bonum* of morality.

Consistent consciousness dovetails with the requirements of a new order that redefines man as an object to be predicted and controlled—a commodity programmed to act in accord with the maxims of capitalism. We find this startling redefinition of man at the foundation of the Adolf Eichmann syndrome. The clue for our analysis comes from de Sade in *Marat/Sade* when he indicts bourgeois revolutions at the close of the eighteenth century:

> and now I see where
> this Revolution is leading
> to the withering of the individual man
> to a slow merging into uniformity
> to a death of choice
> to self denial
> to deadly weakness[6]

These were the unintended results of Kant's Copernican revolution, a revolution that was to set the stage for the extension of capitalist hegemony to consciousness itself. While it is beyond the scope of this paper to present a detailed examination of Kantian philosophy and the Adolf Eichmann syndrome, it is possible to present five rather brash theses on Kant that are intended to foster further discussion and investigation.

1. Human autonomy evaporates in the arid and sterile land-

scape of the First Critique. The autonomous will is but a possibility in the ethereal noumenal realm; in the phenomenal world, the will is externally determined by causes beyond its control (the very essence of alienation). Not only is the will determined; all rational beings (human or otherwise) must structure the world in Newtonian categories. When philosophy is understood as self-confession, it is not surprising that citizens of Königsberg used Kant's punctual daily walks to set their watches.

Kant found the consequences of this rigid determinism abhorrent to his sensibilities since he realized that without autonomy there was no moral responsibility, and he constructed rather specious arguments in the Second Critique to reaffirm freedom of the will. However, although advancing capitalism had little use for noumenal speculations, it could readily pander to hard determinism. This determinism was introjected into popular consciousness to become what C. Wright Mills referred to as "crackpot realism": the doctrine that things cannot be other than what they are. This cynicism is integral to the Adolf Eichmann syndrome, in which aggressors rationalize that they cannot act otherwise, and even if they could, it would make no difference.

Fatalism, however, is not the only implication of Kantian determinism. The very perception of powerlessness itself is a source of aggression that drives the syndrome under discussion. Psychologist Rollo May suggests:

> As we make people powerless, we promote their violence rather than its control. Deeds of violence. . . are performed largely by those trying to establish their self-esteem, to defend their self-image, and to demonstrate that they too are significant.[7]

Triggering the machines of mass destruction is one of the few ways to feel significant in mass society.

2. Kant's epistemological agnosticism generates another component of the syndrome that I call Futilitarian Ethics: the belief that struggle is futile since we cannot know the truth about the world let alone the truth about the morality of our acts. Now

such agnosticism could have become a humanizing force that encouraged tolerance in the face of fallibility. However, in reality, this agnosticism has become a weapon in the ideological arsenal of predatory nations. It encourages a cynical morality in which reactionary and progressive positions seem equally absurd; consider Lafargue's criticism of Kant:

> The workingman . . . knows very well that he is robbed by the employer. . . . Not at all, says the bourgeois sophist whether Hume or Kant. His opinion is personal, an entirely subjective opinion; he might with equal reason maintain that the employer is his benefactor . . . for he cannot know *things-in-themselves*.[8]

Likewise, while the victims of American aggression in Indochina have no trouble making moral judgments about American policy, all too frequently American pilots would excuse themselves by explaining, "I'm only doing my job, and who can say what's right anyway?"

3. The most characteristic feature of both Kantian ethics and the Adolf Eichmann syndrome is unflinching devotion to duty. Of course, Kant did not exhort mankind to obey genocidal order; he merely cautioned us to be rational: that is, be consistent!

This is a purely formal ethic that, in a sense, is value free: any maxim is acceptable as long as it can be consistently legislated. We find this teaching embodied in the syndrome in which the most unspeakable maxim is acceptable as long as it is executed consistently. In fact, to the perpetrators of technological violence, inconsistency, because it is inefficient, is one of the few sins.

The rationality of advanced capitalism generates certain death-dealing maxims that it is our "duty" to follow. Wars are necessary for resources and markets, and this is simply reasonable. Cold warriors are just reasonable men who follow orders, and in the Adolf Eichmann syndrome, "following orders takes away the blame."[9]

4. The architects of technological aggression have adopted Kant's teaching about the priority of duty over passion. A classical criticism of Kant illustrates this denigration of desire: confronted with a man bent on killing our brother, we must tell the

truth about our brother's whereabouts to this man if he asks us, for we cannot consistently legislate lying.

In the Adolf Eichmann syndrome, it is not evil to murder—if that is what duty prescribes—but it is sinful to murder with passion. Passion, of course, puts the warrior in a state of heteronomy with his rational duty. At Nuremberg, Nazis frequently rationalized by insisting that their crimes were not passionate.

The repression of passion has consequences unrecognized by Kant but recognized by many radical Freudians. Repression of life-affirming passion intensifies the death wish, creating a vast reservoir of hostility. The syndrome under discussion may be understood as a way of channeling this hostility into "socially useful" (albeit destructive) behavior. People are conditioned to release aggression through machines, and this conditioning (a) channels hostility into the apparatus of modern warfare and (b) intensifies the aggression; this occurs because such aggression is abstract, vicarious, and frustrating since the original aggression is never fully released.

Marcuse perceives the logic of this process when he explains:

> with the delegation of destruction to an . . . automated thing . . . the instinctual satisfaction of the human person is interrupted, reduced, frustrated, super-sublimated. And such frustration makes for escalation: increasing violence, speed and enlarged scope.[10]

5. Finally, Kant cautions against the recognition of consequences in moral decision making. Likewise, those who direct modern warfare admonish the participants simply to do their duty without regard to consequences. In fact, the very conditions of modern warfare prevent the recognition of consequences by the participants since they engage in activity far removed from its results.

Despite Kant's intentions, he systematized a philosophy that generates the Adolf Eichmann syndrome since it defines man as a powerless object who must be taught to do his duty regardless of feelings or consequences. Unwittingly, Kant reflected the destruction of humane values by the bourgeois revolution, a process aptly described by Marx in the *Communist Manifesto*:

> All fixed, fast-frozen relations, with their train of ancient and venerable prejudices and opinions, are swept away, all new-formed ones become antiquated before they can ossify. All that is solid melts into air, all that is holy is profaned, and man is at last compelled to face with sober senses his real condition of life and his relations with his kind.[11]

How should the Adolf Eichmann syndrome be confronted? Many Marxists argue that it is capitalistic control of ideology that causes us to introject the syndrome; therefore, a Marxist revolution is necessary to depose the ruling class in order to humanize consciousness. Granting that revolution is *necessary*, is it also *sufficient*?

Tacitly assuming the doctrine of economic determinism, many "Marxists" answer "yes" since they hold that a qualitative change in economic conditions will automatically eliminate all pernicious features of the old ideology. But this assumption is fervently denied by both Marx and Engels in several works. Engels, for example, explained:

> Marx and I ourselves are partly to blame for the fact that younger writers sometimes lay more stress on the economic side than is due to it. We had to emphasize this main principle in opposition to our adversaries, who denied it, and we had not always the time, the place or the opportunity to allow the other elements involved to come into their own rights.[12]

These "other elements" are ideologies that persist despite economic revolution due to their antiquity and ubiquity—examples might include racism, sexism, and reactionary religion. Since the mechanical world view can be characterized by its relatively long history as well as its ubiquity, it probably cannot be eradicated by economic revolution alone. This world view can readily be traced back to the seventeenth century, and therefore, few would question its history. But only recently have we become aware of the protean influence of this world view.

The hegemony of Christianity was represented by the cross affixed to every wall and tower. Mechanism has replaced the cross with the clock—the machine that coordinates the entire society for the sake of corporate profit. Kant, in fact, urged that the Newtonian clock-universe was the inevitable structure of consciousness itself.

Mechanism dominates consciousness more efficiently than Christianity does, as witnessed by the way Kant has become common sense: increasingly, ordinary people perceive themselves as unfree victims of forces beyond their control. Cynical and emotionally repressed, they fulfill deeply habituated duties oblivious to the consequences of their actions. This mechanical existence is the very foundation of the Adolf Eichmann syndrome.

It is incorrect to blame Kant for the way his teachings have been historically mediated, and it is incorrect to assume that economic revolution automatically eradicates pernicious ideology. A cultural revolution must occur for us to perceive the world in ways unimagined by Kant.

Autonomy must be reasserted. Of course causality exists, but we ourselves can be causal agents: we can make history by creating new modes of cognition and sensibility, modes that will be instruments of liberation, not domination.

Cynicism must be combated. The Cubans and the Indochinese knew the truth about their material conditions, and they struggled against seemingly overwhelming odds. As philosophers, perhaps our struggle must be against the urbane cynicism that characterizes much of Anglo-American philosophy: "When the Marxist points the finger at reality, the analytic philosopher examines the finger."

Kant reified many of the duties of bourgeois culture by calling them principles of practical reason. These duties must be demystified and redefined as the creations of privileged classes. Who among us would exhort the wretched of the earth not to lie to or steal from their oppressors?

The choice is not between bourgeois duties and nihilism; there also is the possibility of creating truly autonomous individuals legislating mutual obligations. Such autonomy is not the product of simple allegiance to abstract reason; it is the outcome of ending class distinctions in society and the mutual isolation of reason and passion in the person. After such an economic and cultural revolution, duties will become instruments of human fulfillment, not of class domination.

In the meantime, we must combat the sophistry that teaches that following orders takes away the blame.

NOTES

1. Herbert Marcuse, *Negations* (Boston: Beacon Press, 1969), p. 265.
2. Engels to C. Schmidt, 1890, in Karl Marx and Frederich Engels, *The German Ideology*, trans. Lawrence and Wishart (New York: International Publishers, 1972), p. 99.
3. This world view and its dominion over popular consciousness have been ably discussed in works such as Floyd Matson, *The Broken Image* (New York: G. Braziller, 1964); Jurgen Habermas, *Toward a Rational Society* (Boston: Beacon Press, 1970); Sigmund Freud, *Civilization and Its Discontents* (New York: W. W. Norton, 1961); Lewis Mumford, *Art and Technics* (New York: Columbia University Press, 1952); and Jacques Ellul, *The Technological Society* (New York: Vintage, 1964). In the last century, some prophetic visions of the impact of this world view are found in the writings of William Blake, Dostoevsky, and especially in the early works of Marx.
4. Herbert Marcuse, *One Dimensional Man* (Boston: Beacon Press, 1964), p. 104.
5. E. A. Burtt, *The Metaphysical Foundations of Modern Science* (Garden City, N.Y.: Doubleday, 1954), pp. 123-24.
6. Peter Weiss, *The Persecution and Assassination of Marat as Performed by the Inmates of the Asylum of Charenton Under the Direction of the Marquis of Sade*, trans. G. Skelton (New York: Atheneum Press, 1965), p. 38.
7. Rollo May, *Power and Innocence* (New York: W. W. Norton, 1972), p. 23.
8. Quoted by V. I. Lenin in *Materialism and Empirio-Criticism* (Peking: Foreign Language Press, 1972), p. 239. This particular work seems to be premised on a rather mechanistic metaphysics, but in later works, Lenin appears to have modified his position.
9. This line is taken from a song by Phil Ochs, an American folksinger whose works were popular with the New Left in the United States in the mid and late 1960s.
10. Marcuse, *Negations*, p. 263.

11. Karl Marx and Friedrich Engels, *The Communist Manifesto*, in Robert C. Tucker, *The Marx-Engels Reader* (New York: W. W. Norton, 1972), p. 476.

12. Engels to Bloch, 1890, in Tucker, *Marx-Engels Reader*, p. 762.

10
Some Effects of Technology on the Prospects for Peace
GEORGE H. HAMPSCH (USA)

Technological advances have greatly improved the prospects for world peace. These advances, however, also pose both actual and potential dangers to world peace in the foreseeable future, especially as peace is viewed from the vantage point of Marxism.

The most obvious example wherein technology has served the causes of peace is in the area of nuclear weaponry and advanced military technology. Because of the existence of nuclear weapons and advanced conventional weapons, the cost has become excessive in human terms of resolving confrontations between the two ideological systems by means of full-scale war. (Of course, the threat expressed by Premier Khrushchev at the time of the Suez crisis[1] and the much graver threat of President Kennedy at the time of the Cuban missile crisis[2] show clearly that advanced weaponry is by no means a foolproof preventative of wars.)

Moreover, the possession of nuclear weapons and a high degree of military technology allowed the Soviet Union to assume the position of a military superpower in the immediate post-World War II period, long before it had the wherewithal to be considered an economic power capable of challenging the strength of the United States. The ability of the Soviet Union to play the role of a superpower in this period had important strategic consequences for the future of the world. The most significant of these was that it severely limited the options that advanced capitalism had at hand either to undermine existing socialist societies or to prevent the spread of socialism into nonsocialist societies. Few, I believe, would deny the proposition that, if the Soviet Union were not a superpower in the first two decades after World War II, no socialist society would now exist in Eastern Europe (including Yugoslavia and Albania), in East Asia, Cuba, or perhaps even China. Because the Soviet Union was a superpower, the socialist nations were able both to consolidate themselves internally and to expand their influence into the nonsocialist world.

These goals have been accomplished while following a foreign policy based on the principles of peaceful coexistence. These principles are firmly rooted in Marxist-Leninist ideology. They are found consistently and repeatedly in the writings of Lenin.[3] In contemporary times, these principles have been stated on numerous occasions.[4]

The *practical* application of the principles of peaceful coexistence in the form of nuclear pacifism can be traced back at least to the 1962 Cuban missile crisis. From 1962, if not earlier,[5] the Soviet Union and the socialist nations of Eastern Europe have consistently followed a foreign policy designed to avoid a major military confrontation between the two ideological power blocs. The most recent examples (up to the time of this writing) are the reactions of the socialist nations to the intensive bombing of North Vietnam and the mining of the harbor at Haiphong.

This consistent pursuit of a foreign policy of peaceful coexistence has been eminently successful in bringing about the results for which it was designed. It has significantly lessened the danger of major war between nation-states; it has played a major role in bringing about the conditions of détente between major powers of the world; it has, in the process, gently but significantly tipped the balance of geopolitical power in favor of the non-Chinese socialist nations. The Soviet Union and the other socialist countries have done this with utmost diplomatic skill, being most careful to bring about this shift in the balance of power without arousing certain "better-dead-than-red" tendencies that lie dormant in the American psyche.

It simply cannot be denied that there has been a significant shift in the geopolitical balance of power. This is manifested by the *Ostopolitik*, the recognition of the German Democratic Republic (GDR), the convening by the nations of Europe of a European security conference in Helsinki, and the follow-up meetings in Belgrade and Madrid, as well as the SALT talks and the agreement of NATO and the Warsaw Treaty Organization to continue talks on mutual balanced force reductions. There have been important shifts of power in the Persian Gulf, in sub-Sahara Africa, on the subcontinent, in Latin America, and in Southeast Asia. There has been an evident shift of naval power in the Mediterranean, the Indian Ocean, and so on.

Because of this shift in the geopolitical balance, the United States (and incidentally, the People's Republic of China) has been forced to adopt a foreign policy based on the principles of peaceful coexistence. It is true that the United States and the other advanced capitalist powers always have talked in terms of world peace (as Mao continually talked in terms of the "paper tiger" form of peaceful coexistence). But their policies were designed to achieve their political goals at the risk of military confrontation, if necessary. In fact, U.S. foreign policy became more risky as the consistency of the Soviet foreign policy became more evident. Many Americans still feel a sense of pride in recalling the several occasions when the American government was able to call the other side's "bluff" in the "game" of military confrontation. Such events are interpreted as acts of strength and courage on the part of the United States and as acts of either weakness or crude opportunism on the part of the Soviet Union.[6]

It is indeed fortunate that the present leaders of the advanced capitalist world (and China) are realists enough to grasp the new situation and not to cling to their past tendencies to view their ideology in absolutist terms. Fortunately, Western and Chinese leaders have been able to present the shift in foreign policy to their own people and to a large part of the world in terms in which *they* appear to be the initiators of a bold new policy. This may prove to be a danger to world peace in the future, however. At the time of a future world crisis, the American people and their allies may expect the U.S. government to react in its traditionally strong way, yet may suddenly discover that it is unable to do so. At this juncture, the nationalist pride of the American public and pressures from foreign governments may very well force the U.S. government to attempt to resolve the crisis by a threat to intervene with special forces or even to escalate to strategic weapons.[7] Hopefully, the strategists of the socialist world will not overlook this dangerous potentiality. The reaction of the U.S. government and the American people to the Soviet intervention in Afghanistan and to the seizing of American hostages in Iran underscores this danger.

The recent shift in the balance of power has many important implications for the socialist world and for the prospects of peace as seen from the socialist world view. I will mention only two. First, the proletarian states, although they cannot abolish exploitation within the capitalist world, do begin to eliminate the relations of domination and subordination in international affairs. Through peaceful coexistence, the antagonism between bourgeois interests and the proletarian states is so modified that the working class in power is no longer exploited by the international bourgeoisie, which it confronts as an independent force.[8]

Second, the shift of power moves the universal need for general and complete disarmament from the realm of moral ideals more and more toward the realm of practical options. One must not overlook, however, the complexities and contradictory aspects of the process of disarmament.

Obviously, every right-thinking person desires an end to the destructive arms race. Yet it must be recognized that the arms race cannot end as long as there is any serious disparity in the quantity or quality of the military forces of the two major ideological blocs. As soon as a relative parity ("rough equivalency") in military forces and equipment has been reached in any particular arena, then significant moves toward disarmament can begin immediately, as for example, SALT I and II, the Mutual Balanced Force Reduction Talks, and the European Security Conference. Disarmament, short of parity, is a utopian dream. Incidentally, the People's Republic of China has indeed recognized this fact. Its position on general disarmament reflects consistently and clearly the realities of the situation.[9] The Chinese will not consent to disarmament short of either nuclear parity with both the United States and the Soviet Union or else a change in foreign policy by which the goals of the People's Republic and the Soviet Union became unified. Neither appears probable within the foreseeable future; hence, neither does the process of general disarmament.

The Soviet Union also recognizes this principle quite clearly. In those areas in which the United States still has military superiority, as for example in global naval power, the Soviet Union feels itself under no moral imperative to stop its armament preparedness, short of parity.[10] Still, the prospects for disarmament have greatly improved through the shift in geopolitical power.

Since the capitalist world in 1973 more or less accepts the principles of détente as the basis of its foreign policy, the United States, still very much the leader of that world,[11] finds itself with three basic options for foreign policy: (1) to continue the game of power politics between the two superpowers, but without the zero-sum implications that existed during the period of the Cold War;[12] (2) to accept the "five-polar world" model. Here, there is a relinquishing of that type of influence by which the two superpowers hold the political and economic destiny of the world in their hands. This five-polar foreign policy recognizes the interlocking—although unequal—relationships among five power blocs. Through the proper adjustment of these interdependent relationships among the power blocs, a neo-Metternichian or a neo-Bismarckian[13] world order comes into existence. The United States will still attempt to strongly influence the political and economic decisions within this world order, but it will do so in a less visible, more subdued manner.[14] (3) The third option is that of "neoisolationism," or perhaps more correctly, "strategic disengagement." Under this foreign policy schema, the United States voluntarily lessens its political and military influence in the world and attempts to maintain itself as a world power primarily through its worldwide economic presence.[15]

In the foreseeable future, the "five-polar world" policy will indeed prevail, although the "strategic disengagement" position already has had its effect on this multipolar policy. The presence of the United States on the international scene has been relatively subdued in relation to previous periods, although there have been significant pressures to reverse this trend.

Under the multipolar policy, the United States will engage in three separate sets of relationships with three quite different types of nations.[16] First, it basically will be in a competitive relationship with the Soviet Union and China, designed to keep their power in check by utilizing both their mutual hostility and American power and to keep competition under control by cooperating with them on particular measures, especially those necessary to reduce the dangers of war. As the geopolitical balance of power gradually shifts in favor of the socialist forces, U.S. policy will tilt toward China and harden against the Soviet Union.

Second, the United States will engage in a basically cooperative relationship with the other industrially developed nations, Western Europe, Japan, and Canada, in order to deal jointly with the consequences of increasing interdependence, while at the same time allowing the United States to hold its own in the inevitable economic competition with them. This aspect is emphasized especially by the influential "trilateralists."

Third, the U.S. government will engage in relationships with the poor nations of the world designed both to help them develop economically and to mitigate local and regional violence to the extent possible. Thus, it reduces the dangers of both outside involvement and undue dependence on powers that the U.S. government considers hostile to the national interests of the country.

If this indeed becomes the new foreign policy of the United States, then the goals sought by the policy of peaceful coexistence in the capitalist world and in the socialist world are radically different. The United States views peace primarily in terms of world stability, whereas the Soviet Union and the socialist nations view peaceful coexistence in terms of a successful completion of the class struggle.

This divergent interpretation of peaceful coexistence raises both potential and actual dangers to the future of world peace.

Technology will act as a catalyst in precipitating these dangers.

Under conditions of peaceful coexistence, technological advances will tend to undercut the national liberation movements.[17]

Advances in military technology nearly always benefit the counterinsurgents. The war in Vietnam provided an excellent example. A solution in Vietnam was postponed at least from 1965 to 1973 through the introduction of massive firepower, sophisticated weapons, and detection devices.[18]

The advantages that advanced weaponry will give to the counterinsurgents lessen the need for direct intervention by the major capitalist powers and allow for the greater use of indigenous counterinsurgency forces. This changes the sociopsychological character of the struggle and removes the more obvious imperialist connotations. It also increases the insurgents' need for military assistance from the socialist nations.

But perhaps the greatest danger to the national liberation movements comes from the effects that economic technology has on the development of nations. The use of sophisticated modernization techniques allows for a rapid utilization of natural resources in the developing nation with a declining need for imported capital and technical assistance. Direct and obvious intervention into the economy of the developing country by an advanced capitalist power is lessened through the creation of a new educated class of technicians and entrepreneurs. This reduces the stigma of neocolonialism and the stigma attached to the ruling circles. Increased prosperity takes place within the milieu of a strong nationalism. The workers begin to have a vested interest in the status quo. Whatever foreign capital is still needed is primarily in the form of long-term credits funneled into locally owned and controlled enterprises. While these long-term credits can be provided by socialist countries, the vast supply of such available capital is in the hands of the advanced capitalist nations. Granting credits to the developing nations slows the internal development of socialist economies, while the exporting of long-term credits is extremely beneficial to the international bourgeoisie.[19]

Unless one views Marxism in fatalistic terms, it is not inevitable that the developing nations of the world choose the socialist model or even an anti-imperialist stance. They can combine capitalism and nationalist fervor.[20] National "liberation" need not go beyond the breaking of strict colonial-type political ties with the more advanced nations. Exploitation, both internal and external, may continue in a stable, "peaceful" world.

The conditions of peaceful coexistence open up new markets for the unused productive capacities of advanced capitalism, especially those of the United States. It also allows the United States partially to convert its resources from large military production to fulfilling the needs, especially the technological hardware and consumer needs, of the socialist bloc.[21] This is certainly advantageous for peace and for mankind, and, on these grounds alone, no one would object to increased trade. However, there is in this connection a potential danger. The advantages coming to the economy of the United States as a result of the increased trade with socialist countries will help overcome some of the immediate contradictions within the economy of the workers, the farmers, and quite possibly even the poor of the nation. All to the good! Yet the workers may thereby acquire an increased vested interest in the status quo, especially in the world stability that protects the economic status quo. This vested interest may more than offset the increased alienation of the worker in a highly technological society, as well as the disadvantages to him because of the economic struggles between the capitalist powers and because of the internal monetary and economic crises. Workers may perceive their interests to be protected best by identifying with strong nationalist feelings as they arise among the populace at large.

Any Marxist who knows his history should be tremendously impressed by the staying power of capitalism, by its ability to co-opt the labor movement, and by its ability to use the instinctive national loyalties of the workers to weaken the solidarity of the international workers' movement. The socialist world should not underestimate the potential dangers that peaceful coexistence offers for renewing both the economic life of advanced capitalism and the loyalties of the workers to the economies of their respective nation-states.

A second potential danger is to the workers in the socialist states. Détente creates closer cultural, scientific, economic, and political ties between the capitalist world and the socialist world. These may possibly draw socialist workers toward an acceptance of the basic bourgeois world view, with the consequent blurring of class consciousness and the need for class struggle. This danger has been recognized by some of the socialist countries. It was reflected in their strong stand during the preliminary talks to the Conference on Security and Cooperation in Europe, on those clauses dealing with the free flow of persons and ideas between the two ideological systems,[22] as well as in their present interpretation of compliance with its "Basket Three" provisions.

Another potential danger comes from the economic relationships between the socialist world and the developing nations. Through the help given to these nations, economic relationships can result in which the advanced socialist countries are able to benefit economically more fully than the underdeveloped nations. The danger is that the socialist commonwealth may develop a vested interest in maintaining unequal economic relations. In other words, the socialist nations must indeed be on their guard. not to fall into "social-imperialism," that is, a relationship of economic hegemony over certain less prosperous nations due to the need to continually improve the conditions of the workers living under the advanced technology of a developed socialism.

Peaceful coexistence does indeed hold high prospects for a world no longer plagued by armed conflict. For this, mankind is grateful. But the danger that this may result in a fraudulent, false peace also is present. This danger must be recognized and active measures taken to confront it.

The role that technology plays for good or evil is crucial.

NOTES

1. *Khrushchev Remembers*, trans. and ed. Strobe Talbott (Boston: Little, Brown & Co., 1970), pp. 435-36. See also his interview with James Reston, *The New York Times*, October 10, 1957, pp. 1, 10-11, where there is recorded a mild threat against Turkey.

2. Cf. Robert F. Kennedy, *Thirteen Days: A Memoir of the Cuban Missile Crisis* (New York: W. W. Norton & Co., 1969), pp. 108-9, and Jerome H. Kahan and Anne K. Long, "The Cuban Missile Crisis: A

Study of Strategic Context," *Political Science Quarterly* 87, no. 4 (December 1972): 564-90.

3. *Collected Works*, vol. 27, pp. 68-75; vol. 30, pp. 38-39, 50-51, 365-67; vol. 31, pp. 408-15, 487-95; vol. 32, pp. 179-83; vol. 33, pp. 143-55, 162-63, 263-66, 356-57, 383-89; "Interview with Lincoln Eyre," *The World* (February 21, 1920). See also B. Ponomarov, ed., *History of Soviet Foreign Policy* (Moscow: Progress Publishers, 1969), chap. 1-6.

4. The principles of peaceful coexistence were repeated quite clearly at the Bandung Conference of 1955, in the statements of the 20th and 21st Congresses of the CPSU, as well as in the Moscow Declaration and Peace Manifesto of 1957. They were emphasized most strongly in the important Declaration of Representatives of the 81 Communist Parties Meeting in Moscow (November-December, 1960). More recently, the policy of peaceful coexistence has been reiterated in the Report of the 24th Congress of the CPSU and the statement of the CC of the CPSU on the occasion of the 50th anniversary of the Soviet Union. The principles of peaceful coexistence as understood by the Marxist-Leninists are as follows: (1) mutual respect for territorial integrity and sovereignty; (2) mutual nonaggression; (3) noninterference in each other's internal affairs; (4) equality and mutual benefit; (5) respect for all peoples freely to choose their socioeconomic and political systems. Cf. Kurt Erlebach, "Peaceful Coexistence—Political Reality, Form of Class Struggle, Revolutionary factor," *World Marxist Review* 16, no. 2 (February 1973): 43.

5. See *History of Soviet Foreign Policy*, chap. 8-13. A European Security Conference was proposed by the Soviet Union as early as 1954. Cf. Paul Seabury, "On Détente," *Survey* 19, no. 2 (87) (Spring 1973): 70; and Robin Alison Remington, "European Security in the Era of Negotiations," *Current History* 64, no. 381 (May 1973): 220. For the English text of the Soviet note inviting the United States and twenty-three Europeans to such a conference, see *New Times* (Moscow: November 13, 1954), 46, p. 3.

6. On this point, see Christopher Leman, "Must We Always Be Tough?" *Foreign Policy*, no. 11 (Summer 1973): 93-101.

7. See David Watt, "Four More Years—Of What?" *Foreign Policy*, no. 9 (Winter 1972-73): 9.

8. Erlebach, "Peaceful Coexistence," p. 43.

9. Chiao Kuan-hua, "Soviet Disarmament Proposal Is a Fraud," *Peking Review* 15, no. 46 (November 17, 1972): 5-6; Lin Peng, "Remarks to a Plenary Meeting of the Third United Nations Conference on Trade and Development," quoted in "Chinese Comment on Soviet Foreign

Policy," compiled by the Subcommittee on National Security and International Operations of the Committee on Government Operations, U.S. Senate (Washington, D.C.: U.S. Government Printing Office, 1972), pp. 7-8.

10. L. I. Brezhnev, Speech of June 1971, as quoted in G. Soyatov and A. Kokoshin, "Naval Power in the U.S. Strategic Plans," *International Affairs* (Moscow: April 1973), p. 62.

11. Cf. Raymond Vernon, "Rogue Elephant in the Forest," *Foreign Affairs* 51, no. 3 (April 1973): 573-87.

12. Eugene V. Rostow, *Peace in the Balance* (New York: Simon & Schuster, 1972), especially chap. 10.

13. See Zbigniew Brzezinski, "U.S. Foreign Policy: The Search For Focus," *Foreign Affairs* 51, no. 4 (July 1973): 715; and James Chace, *A World Elsewhere* (New York: Charles Scribner's Sons, 1973), pp. 28-35.

14. Seyom Brown, "The Changing Essence of Power," *Foreign Affairs* 51, no. 2 (January 1973): 286-99; George F. Kennan, "After the Cold War," *Foreign Affairs* 51, no. 1 (October 1972): 210-27. The five powers are, of course, the United States, the Soviet Union, Western Europe, China, and Japan.

15. Earl C. Ravenal, "The Case for Strategic Disengagement," *Foreign Affairs* 51, no. 3 (April 1973): 505-21; Robert W. Tucker, *A New Isolationism: Threat or Promise?* (New York: Universe Books, 1972); Daniel Yergin, "Fulbright's Circle," *Worldview* 16, no. 2 (February 1973): 7-13.

16. William J. Barnds, "Nixon's America After Vietnam," *Worldview* 16, no. 4 (April 1973): 5. See also, "National Security Policy and the Changing World Power Alignment," Report by the Subcommittee of National Security Policy and Scientific Developments, Committee on Foreign Affairs, U.S. House of Representatives, October 25, 1972. (Washington, D.C.: U.S. Government Printing Office, 1972), pp. 3-6.

17. The forces of the ultra-Left have clearly recognized this danger. As a result, they have condemned the policy of peaceful coexistence, at least in the manner it has been practiced by the leading Socialist countries. See for example, D. Horowitz, "Nixon's Vietnam Strategy: How It Was Launched with the Aid of Brezhnev and Mao and How the Vietnamese Intend to Defeat It," *Ramparts* 11, no. 2 (August 1972): 17-20.

18. It also is obvious that the solution in Cambodia was delayed by the use of massive firepower and sophisticated weapons. Cf. William P. Rogers, Secretary of States, Testimony before the U.S. Senate Foreign Relations Committee, *The New York Times*, May 1, 1973, p. 10.

19. Lynn Turgeon, "Address to the National Conference on American Policy Toward the Two German States," held at New York City, June

3, 1972 (New York: American Society for the Study of the German Democratic Republic, 1972). See however, G. Skorov, " 'Transfer of Technology' and Neocolonialist Manoeuvres," *International Affairs* no. 5 (Moscow: May 1972): 55-62.

20. Of the thirteen nations comprising the important Organization of Petroleum Exporting Countries (OPEC), only three (Iraq, Libya, and Algeria) have socioeconomic systems in any way resembling the socialist model.

21. Turgeon, "Address to the National Conference." See also, Seymour Melman, *Pentagon Capitalism* (New York: McGraw-Hill, 1970), especially pp. 71-96 and 184-205.

22. Joseph Harned et al., "Conference on Security and Cooperation in Europe and Negotiations on Mutual and Balanced Force Reductions," *The Atlantic Community Quarterly* 11, no. 1 (Spring 1973): 11-14, 43. See also V. Knyazhinsky, "Détente and the Problems of Ideological Struggle," *International Affairs* no. 4 (Moscow: April 1973): 17-18; B. Kudinov and V. Pletnikov, "Ideological Confrontation of the Two Systems," ibid., no. 12 (December 1972), pp. 60-61; Jack F. Matlock, "US-Soviet Relations in the 1970's," *Survey* 19, no. 2 (Spring 1973): 136; Jean de Madre, Preface to C. A Dake, *Impediments to the Free Flow of Information Between East and West* (Paris: Atlantic Treaty Association, 1973).

11
Discussion and Replies 1

V. V. SHELIAG (USSR)

I requested the floor to express the viewpoint of Soviet Marxists on the question being discussed here, of philosophers' attitudes to the problem of war and peace. In this hall and in almost all sections of the congress, this problem has been repeatedly referred to, and I think that, apart from the sincere desire to prevent war, there were expressions of views that should be reacted to, that should be opposed because sometimes our Marxist positions are being misinterpreted. Yesterday a speaker alleged that we divide wars into good and bad. I must emphatically reject such a charge against the Soviet Marxists, who believe all wars to be bad. We believe there are just and unjust wars, but this is quite a different matter. Marxists believe that wars are an extreme way, an extreme means of resolving political matters, and they resort to this means only when they are forced to do so by their class enemy. Our October socialist revolution developed from the very beginning in such a way as to avoid bloodshed. This is what Lenin appealed for. If we did not manage to avoid bloodshed, the blame for this is to be laid at the door of our enemy, our people's enemies.

Mr. Chairman, dear colleagues, we seem to have disregarded one circumstance. We here had a most ardent discussion of nuclear war. But war without the use of nuclear weapons also is a dangerous thing. The scientific and technological revolution led to the development not only of nuclear weapons but also to a colossal development of the means of destruction of human life that nevertheless remains within the limits of what are termed conventional weapons. If we compare these two kinds of weapons, we shall see that in ten years of war in Vietnam the American armed forces dropped on that country thirty million tons of explosives. If we are talking about equivalents, this would equal 650 atomic bombs of the type dropped on Hiroshima. Would it be possible to believe that the Vietnamese children who died under the American conventional bombs were happier than the Japanese children who died under the American atomic bombs?

I don't want you to understand me in the sense that I am trying to rehabilitate atomic war. That would be far from the truth. I share most views on the global danger of this kind of war with the exception of the extreme views on the final end of civilization. Our task is not to establish the dosage of military weapons; that is the task of the strategists. Our task is to advance a general attitude toward war. Our principled position as Marxists is to reject war as a way of solving urgent problems, and this is where our views partly coincide with those of the pacifists. But we differ from pacifists on two points. We cannot accept the position they are trying to persuade us of: that we should reject war in general. Yesterday at a round table, one of the philosophers said that love could solve our problems and, more particularly, that one should love one's enemy. A Bulgarian comrade answered him: "How, then, can we love the victim of the aggression? You are teaching us to love the aggressor himself."

We cannot recommend to people fighting for their liberty to give up war. The forces of aggression have weapons and use them; they use them every time they think it fitting to do so. The tragic experience of Chile testifies to this. Obviously, lessons will be drawn from this in many countries, but I would like to say just one thing: the Chilean revolution was put down because it failed to use, or didn't want to use, its own force in opposition to the force of reaction. The man elected by the people, President Allende, a hero and a martyr, was shot down by officers who remain unknown. This is a cruel lesson that shows how right Lenin was when he said that a revolution, if it wants to win, must know how to defend itself. We want to defend our revolution; we know how to do so; we have the means to do so.

Our second difference from pacifists consists in the fact that we do not confine ourselves to mere condemnations or to appeals to change the nature of man so that we can eliminate the war instinct, because we know that the nature of man is determined by social conditions. We do everything possible to prevent wars. This is shown by our policy of peace and is known to everybody. It is shown by our efforts everywhere to prevent war, efforts that have led to real possibilities of avoiding a thermonuclear war, a missile war.

A great deal has been said about just and unjust wars at this congress, and some have questioned the very formulation of the problem. Criteria are necessary, and Marxism-Leninism has worked out such criteria. Whether we can consider a war to be just or unjust rests on the answers to these questions: In whose interest, of which class, is the war being waged? What forces are waging the war? Is the war defending a just cause or is it serving the interest of reaction, of trying to bring oppression back? Is it trying to liberate the people, or trying to perpetuate a colonial rule? I can't go into any further detail, but these criteria would be roughly sufficient to determine whether a war is just or unjust, whether or not it is a predatory, aggressive war. And on this will depend the attitude of the masses of the people toward it and the way it will affect them.

The question of war as a continuation of politics is today assuming ever greater urgency. A proof of this is the fact that not only Marxists but anti-Marxists draw attention to this problem, and that many different conclusions have been drawn concerning war as a continuation of politics. Sometimes we witness a logic of shifting terms, of illicit substitution of concepts, which is not merely an error of logic but is a deliberate attempt to justify the politics of imperialism.

Let me explain briefly how this kind of logical error comes about. There are two notions found in the literature on this question. One is that war is a continuation of politics by means of violence. The second raises the issue: Is it fitting nowadays to use war as a means for the continuation of politics? These two things sound more or less the same, but they are quite different. The second notion suggests that a time will come when the socialist revolution will prevail throughout the world and that war will not be necessary. But wars are inherent in a class society. They are a continuation of the politics of classes—either the different classes within one state or the ruling classes of different states. This is a basic position that was expressed by Lenin when he used the formula of Clausewitz. But Lenin invested it with a different meaning because Clausewitz believed politics to be the free will of the ruler, whereas Lenin and his disciples believe politics to be an expression of the interest of the ruling class. When it is said that under present-day conditions it is not possible to use war as a continuation of politics because of the destructive character of thermonuclear war, we can agree with this because the Soviet Union does not consider that it has to achieve its political aims by way of war.

Our communist purpose, our program of building a communist society, is best implemented in conditions of peace. We are convinced that conditions of peace make the best atmosphere, the best setting for the development of social progress in all countries. Both in advanced capitalist countries and in the developing countries, such progress would ultimately lead to the triumph of socialism and communism throughout the world, without war. We are in favor of such a world development, and we are trying to promote it. By means of war under the present conditions of the existence of nuclear weapons and missiles, the imperialists cannot achieve their aims, no matter what they are, because if they unleash a war they will be destroyed in that war, and we believe they will be destroyed as the result of the operation of the political forces in their countries, which will mature in the course of the war, for we know war is a teacher, and the military defeat of imperialism would be significant, too. We do not deny or reject the formulation to the effect that, under present conditions, there is no sense in trying to achieve political aims by means of war.

However, this doesn't mean that we limit the possibility or the chances of a war of national liberation because, if there are no other means that can be used, a war of national liberation should be waged. But we agree that, given the weaponry of the present day, we should not and do not want to achieve political objectives by those means. And we are not giving up the class concept of the nature of war. There are reactionary groups that call the Soviet Union and the socialist countries their presumptive enemies. This was done by certain political functionaries quite recently. If we, including philosophers, do not manage to stop these insane people, and a war should start, it could not be anything but the continuation, on the part of imperialism, of a criminally aggressive politics. On our part, it would be a continuation of the politics of the construcion of a society of peace, progress, and socialism. I would like to ask you to understand me: we are not in favor of trying to achieve our aims by means of war. We are doing everything possible to avoid war, and we hope that we will manage to prevent it.

Just one comment concerning the contribution by—I'm sorry I haven't the name here—about the contraditions between China and the Soviet Union as contradictions in the socialist world. Marxism is not to blame for the disagreements and conflicts between the Soviet Union and China. Socialism as a system is not to blame for them. These conflicts arose in connection with the fact that certain Chinese leaders have deviated from Marxism. If certain people hope that these conflicts will escalate into a war, we must disappoint them. The Soviet Union is pursuing a confident and calm policy, and we have hopes based on the reason and good sense of the great Chinese people, with whom we have lived in peace, whom we helped toward the victory of their socialist revolution, and who, we hope, will not allow the antisocialist tendencies appearing in certain fields of Chinese political life to gain dominance.

F. T. KONSTANTINOV (USSR)

The teachings of Marxism-Leninism are always alive and constantly developing along with the development of human society, the class struggle, and socialism. These teachings are developing creatively. Marx and Engels, as is well known, turned socialism from utopianism into science. Lenin and our party, which was founded by him, together with the Soviet people, turned socialism not only into a scientific theory but also into everyday social practice. We have confirmed the correctness of the Marxist-Leninist teaching and have provided conditions for its future creative development. This task is being fulfilled today by the joint activities of the Marxist parties, as seen in the documents of the communist movement.

In the documents of the party congresses, we find answers to the vital questions posed by the development of socialism. We cannot even enumerate all the problems that have been elaborated by our Marxist-Leninist party, the whole range of problems involved in advanced socialist society, in the development of nations constituting a new type of historical community, such as the Soviet nations.

The fact that Marxist-Leninist teachings will live and develop now and in the future is evident in the conditions of such a problem as war and peace. Marxism has always emphasized the role of the masses. Even though wars are started by the exploiting classes, the masses carry out the wars. This idea was creatively developed, and we can see now how the role of the masses is constantly growing—in culture, in education, and in the struggle for peace. In this connection, I would like to propose that we should discuss not only the role of the masses in the struggle for peace but also their responsibility for the safeguarding of peace.

Here, our esteemed chairman, John Somerville, very rightly spoke of what future nuclear war can bring to humanity. If we made a sort of agreement during the Cuban missile crisis, it does not mean that we were afraid. We were well aware that this was blackmail directed against the Soviet Union. And if war was avoided, as it was, the only reason is that the Soviet Union, the Marxists, manifested not only flexibility but also firmness in their decisions in defense of peace. The fact that we are now living in the conditions of peace is the continuing result of this flexibility and firmness.

Let me emphasize, as I said, not only the role but also the responsibility of the masses of people. Nowadays, if a war breaks out, it will not be possible, as it was previously, to punish only those who started it. In the kind of devastation that would be produced by the use of nuclear weapons, many many more besides the warmongers will suffer, including those who have placed their destinies in the hands of their leaders. That is why we philosophers, scientists, and humanists should deal with these problems. We should raise the question of the possibility of nuclear war. Even though I think the possibility that nuclear war would actually be fought is very slight, it cannot be wholly excluded. Our effectiveness, however, the effectiveness of our struggle will grow if the responsibility of the masses of people also will grow.

We can confidently state that in a socialist country the destiny of peace and the future is protected by the Communist party, which is the representative of the peace-loving forces. Thus, we can confidently state that the Soviet Union will never begin a nuclear war. In his presentation, Academician Fedoseyev said that wars can be just and unjust. If the Soviet Union were attacked, if imperialism should strike, we would have to retaliate. These problems of peace and war deserve the attention that is devoted to them, and I am sure that in our future discussions we will be able to make our contribution to the common cause of safeguarding peace and socialism.

E. E. MODRZHINSKAIA (USSR)

The problems of war and peace that were discussed here are especially important to all of us. History testifies to this fact, for in the two world wars started by imperialism, three and a half times more lives were lost than in all the wars of the previous one hundred years. In the eighteenth century, three million persons were killed in wars, but in World War II alone, the monstrous Hitlerite aggression resulted in the loss of twenty million lives in the Soviet Union alone. Fourteen million dead was the total for the three preceding centuries, while twenty million were killed in World War II in one country alone! It is not surprising, therefore, that Soviet scholars and Soviet leaders, the vanguard of our country, and the entire Soviet people take to heart the question of the struggle for peace.

The theoretical elaboration of these problems and, first of all, practical steps toward safeguarding world peace—that is the policy and the line of our country—the policy of peaceful coexistence. This policy was announced by Lenin only two days after the establishment of the Soviet power—November 8, 1917 —and it has been resolutely, unswervingly pursued by our country ever since.

I would like to call attention to two questions in this connection. The first concerns the indissoluble relation between the wise and humanistic policy of peaceful coexistence, on the one hand, and social progress, on the other. Only from the standpoint of this connection can we approach our problems scientifically. Neither the theoretical nor the practical problems of the struggle for peace should be separated from the important human and scientific problems of social progress. What is the nature of this strong relationship between the struggle for peace and the interests of social progress?

The first thing that must be observed is that the conditions of peaceful coexistence are the most favorable conditions for the progress of advanced social formations, that is, socialist formations, the socialist community that exists in reality. And in spite of the great difficulties, and the monstrous, barbarous destruction of World War II inflicted by fascism, the people of the socialist countries have successfully continued to develop their national economies, culture, and science, so that now there is an inviolable fortress that can safeguard world peace. Thus, the fact that peaceful coexistence offers the best conditions for the construction of socialism and communism is the essence of its relation to social progress.

The second point is that under the conditions of peaceful coexistence, which makes illegal the interferences and aggressions of reactionary forces, conditions are created for every nation to be master in its own house and to create the political and economic order that will correspond to the interests of the people. Such principles as noninterference in the internal affairs of others, sovereignty, the right of self-determination, and the implementation of these principles in international agreements will no doubt contribute to the further improvement of the possibilities of peace and progress. This will help the general development of humankind. Moreover, peaceful coexistence brings about opportunities that facilitate mutually profitable economic and cultural contacts for promoting social progress, provided these contacts are not used to subvert and erode the building of socialism or to damage the interest of either party. Cultural links that promote friendship among peoples can only strengthen peace, and we heartily support such links.

The question of ideology also was raised here. What happens to ideology, to the ideological struggles and class struggles under conditions of peaceful coexistence? What happens to the struggle for national liberation? To think these things would cease to exist would mean that one is taking a nonscientific approach, for nothing can stop the movement of mankind along the road of progress. And what actually is ideology? It is the theoretical and systematized level of social consciousness, the level that reflects, as any social thinking does, the level of social reality. And as long as there are on the planet two systems of social reality contradictory in their social interests, and antagonistic classes that confront each other, there will be conflicts of ideology.

But this kind of conflict should be conducted on a plane in which frankness and truth prevail. That is why we oppose slander, defamation, and other such tactics in ideological struggles, tactics that have been directed against the socialist countries, especially against the Soviet Union. We reject with indignation such slanders and distortions, which have even been used in relation to the leading truths of socialism. This is a problem that calls for the recognition of such a scientific fact as the existence of two conflicting ideologies. Science, however, is on the side of our ideology because ours is a scientific ideology. It differs deeply and qualitatively from the ideology that confronts us. I believe that in such serious meetings as this one should be completely frank.

A further point is that the struggle for peace poses a number of important new questions. For example, even though the overwhelming majority of humanity is undoubtedly for peaceful coexistence, there are reactionary circles in opposition to it, some supported by the military-industrial complex. In addition, there are various neofascist organizations. No matter how destructive the impact of fascist war was, the fascists are still against peaceful coexistence, and they promulgate slanderous, misleading arguments against our line of thought. We believe that a struggle must be waged against the ideological represenatives of such reactionary forces and that the forces of peaceful coexistence should be further strengthened.

Other aspects of the struggle for peaceful coexistence include efforts to oppose unscientific and irrational ideas about the causes of war. For example, some scholars, in theory and practice, back a regulatory approach to conflicts. They are not warmongers, but they have erroneous notions concerning the reasons for and causes of war. Let us consider briefly some of the most widespread of these notions. A number of Western theoreticians think that human nature, the very nature of man, makes war inevitable since this nature is inherently aggressive. We maintain that this is an erroneous position, and we have taken pains to demonstrate its falsity in our books and articles. Among other erroneous positions is the claim that international anarchy is the cause of war so that a world government must be set up. We think this also is a mistaken idea because in practical politics this notion leads to reactionary positions that prevent nations struggling for national independence to implement their sovereign rights. This would mean that we should limit the rights of peoples to express their will freely and to organize their social order in accordance with their will. We do not agree with this theory.

We have a book, *Problems of War and Peace*, which is available here. It has been translated into English, and in it we try to make our views known. We criticize these theories and ideas from a scientific standpoint and make clear why we regard them as ungrounded. We believe that interested scholars from different countries should get together and exchange their views and opinions.

In conclusion, we appeal to the social scientists from different countries to carry out their great responsibilities for peace and social progress. This also involves the right of every people to set up a social system that may facilitate its development from capitalism to socialism. We feel that this is the essence of our time. Many assert that now is the era of the scientific and technological revolution. This revolution is an important phenomenon, but the essence of our era is the underlying development from capitalism to socialism, that is, toward a more progressive social order, and it is along this road that the most complex problems are being solved in practice.

It is in this fact that the deep humanism of socialism consists. Our humanism is not simply verbal but is expressed in our deeds, in the struggle for social and national liberation, in the struggle for the strengthening of peace and against the devastation of a nuclear war. These are the tasks that have been marked out by the vanguard of the communist movement. And that is why the army of the peace-loving forces grows by the hour. That is why nothing else but the strengthening of peace and socialism can be a criterion of humanism. That is why we should work actively for the all-around development of the human personality in order to obtain ever more favorable conditions for the material, spiritual, and cultural development of every member of society. And this is what the Soviet people and the people of the other socialist countries are doing.

It seems to me that it is the task of social scientists and other scholars to study the experience of mankind, not only the experience of war, suffering, and deprivation, but also the experience and the practice of actual, living socialism. It would be excellent if we could meet more often and if such excellent symposia as this one were organized more often. I believe that our meeting here will contribute greatly both to social progress and to the strengthening and defending of peace throughout the world.

E. HERLITZIUS (GDR)

I want to refer first to what Ronald Hirschbein called the Adolf Eichmann syndrome; second to the problem of a "planetary ecology" within a planetary environment, mentioned by Howard Parsons; and third to the concluding remarks that John Somerville made last Wednesday in regard to whether or not there is any urgent reason to insist on making a qualitative distinction between a war fought with conventional weapons and one fought with thermonuclear weapons—as far as the Marxist-Leninist theory on war and peaceful coexistence is concerned.

To my first remark: Hirschbein gives the name "Eichmann syndrome" to the kind of intellectual cynicism that is produced when an aggression is rationalized and "when all too many people witness, condone, and commit international atrocities with little apparent emotional involvement or moral responsibility." Indeed, Eichmann's name—along with other names—personifies fascist crimes. But it is a matter of indifference whether the cruelties are committed face to face or have been ordered from neat desks. All those in my country who have learned their lesson of history know very well what the root of this evil is. Eichmann's crimes germinated out of a social and economic formation that, in the totality of socially transmitted behavior patterns, was imbued with militarism and, likewise, with officially inspired opposition to progress.

As far as the decay of morals on such a large scale is concerned, neither a single individual nor a traditional ideology can be blamed in analyzing the causes of this process. It is the social basis of such cruelties that must be analyzed.

Thus, the roots of such crimes as Eichmann's are found in the social relations of the imperialist stage of capitalism, and they become the less effective the more the struggle for peace and for a real democracy becomes successful.

It seems to me that the category "syndrome" serves to camouflage the true causes. It is a mere dealing with superficial phenomena if nothing but an "unflinching devotion to duty," to duty as such, is taken into account. Who gives orders, for whom, what for, in which society? That is the question. Is it a society that breeds war, or is it a society that uses order and authority in the interest of the majority, in the interest of the working people at home and abroad?

It has been outlined in the papers of our colleagues from the Soviet Union, and in the contributions of the participants from other socialist countries, how we strive for the fully developed human being, educated in the spirit of universal concerns. But the situation we nowadays still live in leaves no doubt that Hirschbein is wrong when he says that the autonomy of the individual should depend on "the outcome of *ending* class distinctions in society." If the Communist party of the Soviet Union and such brave Communists as Dimitroff had not made a scientific Marxist-Leninist analysis of fascism and based it on the theory of class struggle, all Germans could easily have been condemned along with those who were found guilty at the Nuremberg trials. I think the United States then took the same position.

Second, a short remark on Parsons' claim for securing a planetary environment. I agree with him, that this problem is depressing us more and more. But I must raise an objection against his empiricism and insist on the fact that a theoretical base does exist. Nothing else but Marx's theory of intensified widened reproduction gives us the key to analyze the qualitatively different conditions of man in his relation to nature. It is up to the working people in the capitalist countries to control and reduce the reckless exploitation of nature, to stop the pollution of water and air practiced by the monopolies, and to cooperate in all possible fields with the socialist states in further developing the policy of peaceful coexistence. But if we say that a "planetary ecology" should become predominant over all other sociological and theoretical notions of Marxism, that we should maintain an indefinite theory of a universal environment instead of giving a profound analysis of the drive for profit and the exploitation of labor, then the main ecological problems of the world at the present time could not be analyzed at all.

Please allow me to note in that connection Marx's following words:

> One capitalist always kills many. Hand in hand with this centralization, or this expropriation of many capitalists by few, develop, on an ever extending scale, the co-operative form of the labor process, the conscious technical application of science, the methodical cultivation of the soil, the transformation of the instruments of labor into instruments of labor usable only in common, the economizing of all means of production by their use as the means of production of combined, socialized labor . . . but with this, too, grows the revolt of the working

class, a class always increasing in numbers, and disciplined, united, organized by the very mechanism of the process of capitalist production itself. The monopoly of capital becomes a fetter upon the mode of production. . . .[1]

However, the most urgent problem is this one: whether or not there is a need to change our Marxist point of view about the character of wars after the threat of thermonuclear war has come up. I appreciate Somerville's engagement in our mutual struggle for peace. But the unity in deciding the next practical steps is only one side of the coin; the call for a wholly new theory is the other side. Before Marxists change such a conception as the theory on just and unjust wars, they must certainly ask whom it serves most.

It seems to me that the main reason for Somerville's proposal concerning the concept of just and unjust wars is his intention of uniting the whole world under conditions of détente in peaceful coexistence. And his far-reaching intention to stress what the enlarged danger of a thermonuclear war for mankind really means, needs support. And to that extent, I go along with him in calling special attention to the qualitative change in the scale of destructiveness of modern warfare. But reasoning from such a scale of increased destructiveness, the bombing of Vietnam alone adduces proof.

Let me ask what, in our striving to prevent thermonuclear war, could be more useful than following Lenin's line that the main thing is to *disclose the very secret in which the unjust wars of today, the imperialist wars, are born*? Evidently, no thermonuclear war, no war at all will ever be *started* by the community of socialist states—that is what all speakers of the Wednesday discussion agreed on. This is even the experience of 1962. And as Debiprasad Chattopadhyaya has stated here, the socialist world never showed any interest in the actual use of the thermonuclear weapons even in the moment of gravest provocation. Evidently, the danger comes only from one side: from the imperialist system.

Thus, it is absolutely necessary to raise the fundamental question of the class character of war: the relation of the commercial and political interests, of the military-industrial complex, to the origin of a war, and how the forces of peace could be marshaled under the leadership of the working class to disclose all the secrets of preparing a war and how to prevent it.

This means that the thermonuclear aggression, even in any preparatory stage, is to be branded unjust, is to be judged as the continuation of imperialist politics. Therefore, we have to declare that a thermonuclear war is not a new type of war as far as its class character is concerned; it could only be regarded as an unjust imperialist war.

And finally, let me point out what could happen if we were to abandon our Marxist-Leninist analysis of just and unjust wars. Take, for instance, the Israeli imperialist aggression against the Arab states, which was condemned by the United Nations in 1967. To impress this fact on the consciousness of the people of the world as unjust by international law means to strengthen the peace forces and to recall the aggressor, *possibly without a further war*. Moreover, India, Pakistan, and Bangladesh have had experience of this kind in reducing the incidence of local or national war.

Hirschbein, as the first speaker this morning, asked what our moral position concerning the use of thermonuclear weapons should be. And in his answer, he disqualified the Marxist criteria as outdated. I don't think that the question of the working people can be outdated, this very essential question: out of what is war born? It would be a dangerous skepticism to give mere emotional warnings and to escape from saying what the "new morality" conerning war and peace should be. I am sure that such a morality must be useful as a tool to prevent imperialist wars right at the beginning.

A new morality—it does exist! Look at the forces struggling for peace in the whole world: look at the peoples of the socialist states; look at Vietnam! Look at our wonderful young generation; look at the students I have the honor to teach!

K. T. FANN *(Canada)*

First of all, I would like to express my appreciation for John Somerville's tremendous work in bringing together this first international philosophical discussion of war and peace in view of the technological revolution.

At this point, let me emphasize that I think we should distinguish between different kinds of war. A lot of attention is being paid to nuclear war, to the possibility of world nuclear war. But there are wars of national liberation, revolutionary civil wars, and even the possibility of other kinds of wars—wars between supposedly socialist nations. Let me try to analyze each kind of war and express my opinion of it from the Marxist-Leninist point of view, that is, how we should regard it. But Somerville's position is that, because of the technological revolution and the new weaponry, we should change our attitudes and conceptions about war, and that the prevention of nuclear war is the precondition of the solution of any other problem. I disagree with this thesis. It is true that the nature of world war is changing because of the tremendous destructiveness of nuclear weapons. But it also is true that, because the capitalists no longer possess a monopoly of nuclear arms, a new world war has so far been prevented.

At the same time, there has been a lot of discussion, for example, of the nuclear confrontation during the Cuban missile crisis. We are told to draw the lesson of it and to draw new moral values from it. I do not see that Marxists have any lesson to learn from the Cuban missile crisis except this, namely, after committing opportunism, Khrushchev was forced to capitulate. That is the only lesson. We all know that the capitalists are engaged in nuclear blackmail and that they are the only ones engaged in nuclear blackmail. Socialist countries should possess nuclear weapons, and the only reason for their possessing nuclear weapons is to prevent that blackmail. Socialist countries should declare publicly that they would never be the first to use nuclear weapons. And they should never engage in any kind of nuclear gambling, such as the placing of nuclear missiles in Cuba, nor should they engage in any kind of nuclear provocation.

The facts of history have shown that the emergence of nuclear weapons has not changed the nature of imperialism or capitalism, although it has changed the nature of world war. Now we can assume that either the imperialists are completely insane or they are not. If they are insane enough to unleash the nuclear weapons, then there is nothing we can do; there is simply nothing we can do. However, my assumption is that they are not insane, that they have a logic of their own: the capitalists look after their class interests.

History since the emergence of nuclear weapons has shown that U.S. imperialism is perfectly capable of understanding the nuclear reality, and in fact, Americans have prepared themselves to engage in special warfare, such as that in Korea and Vietnam, and to intervene directly in many other places. The history of such interventions is a mixed one. In certain places, the imperialists have actually been stopped. In other places, they have been very successful in their interventions and counterrevolutionary movements, for example, in the Dominican Republic, in Indonesia, in Greece, and in Chile.

What concerns me is that, in all this talk about changing conceptions of war, we have to be clear about whom we are talking to. Are we talking to the imperialists and aggressors, or are we talking to the socialists and the oppressed? Oppressed nations and oppressed peoples do not possess nuclear arms. It is imperialism that possesses nuclear arms and engages in nuclear blackmail. If we can convince imperialists to change their minds, then we should talk to them, and not request the oppressed nations and peoples to change their conceptions about war and peace because of the emergence of nuclear weapons. They are not the violators of peace; in fact, they are the defenders of world peace.

Now with regard to national liberation and revolutionary civil wars, the reality of the world shows that if a form of oppression and a system of exploitation of man by man exists, wars will continue. This is the objective evaluation of the situation, regardless of our wishes against war and for peace. But our preference in favor of peace is not going to change imperialism: it is not going to change the exploitative system of capitalism. The only way to change that is through people's war, the national liberation movement, and the class struggle within the capitalist nations. In this sense, I think that wars have increased since the emergence of nuclear weapons, and here we have lessons to learn.

I have in mind two examples, first of all that of Vietnam. Here we have a case of true humanism winning against the so-called technological revolution, the tremendous technology in the hands of imperialists, the misuse of this technology by imperialism. The basic Marxist principle of people liberating themselves and making history is not changed by the technological revolution. That for me remains valid.

Second, let us look at the tragic example of Chile. I think all socialists wish and hope for the possibility of a peaceful transition to socialism through legal and political means. But in the whole history of mankind, we have not seen a single example to show that this is possible. At the beginning ten years ago, we all had high hopes that it would be possible in Chile, and it might have been possible if Chile had been left alone. But we live in a world of international imperialism. Imperialism intervened with an economic blockade and sabotage to subvert that revolution. The lesson that Marxists can learn is that, although we struggle for a peaceful transition, we should always be prepared for armed struggle. The armed forces in each society are always an instrument of oppression at the disposal of the ruling class. The lesson we learn from Chile is that a socialist may be elected into the government but that there is a distinction between the government and the state. The state is in the hands of the ruling class within the country and also may be in the hands of foreign capital. The *government* may *temporarily* be in the hands of the working class, but unless you can destroy or in some way neutralize the armed forces of the ruling class, the revolution cannot succeed.

Now third and finally, I would like to come to the question of the antagonistic relationships between the supposedly socialist nations. Very ironically, the antagonism between China and the Soviet Union has become one of the most immediate threats to world peace. Most of our speakers have referred to the socialist camp as opposed to the capitalist camp, as if there were one unified socialist camp (perhaps they do not include China at all in their term "socialist camp"). But the fact is that now Marxists and socialists are faced with a real problem as regards war and peace—the possibility of armed conflict or war between the socialist nations. I am surprised that in this colloquium, where we are discussing the problems of war and peace, none of us has discussed this very urgent and imminent question—probably the only question on which the persons here have influence and can do something about. There is nothing we can do about imperialism, nothing we can do about the armed struggle in which the oppressed people in the third world are engaged. No amount of our talk will change their minds. They will liberate themselves. The only place in which we can really be effective is the realm of the conflict between the two largest socialist nations, but we are not addressing that question.

I myself have no solution, but I want to point out that we are facing a new situation with regard to the question of war and peace. We Marxists should engage ourselves in that situation—analyze it, discuss it. We should try to be active and helpful, first in defusing the possibility of armed conflict among the socialist nations and second in contributing to the possibility of bringing about a unity among the socialist nations in the face of the common enemy, imperialism.

FRANZ LOESER (GDR)

Let me preface my comment with a somewhat personal remark. Well do I remember how, during those years when I lived in emigration, I dreamed of the day when my country, Germany, would be free from fascism, and we would be able to build socialism. And I thought at that time that once the working class had power the other problems in our country would be relatively simple. After all, our Marxist party would be in power, the power of the capitalist class would be broken, and we would all be struggling for the same thing and the same goals. So, what problems could there really be? Well, the delegates from the socialist countries will agree with me that such a view is naive and that the building of socialism is an extremely difficult thing. We know even more. We know that year by year the problems on the road to communism become more and more difficult.

Thus, it is not surprising that here at this colloquium we have, among Marxists who are all agreed on the basic principles in the writings of Marx, Engels, and Lenin, significant differences in relation to some very important questions. I disagree with a number of speakers on different things. Let me take as an example the remarks made by K. T. Fann on the Cuban missile crisis and the policy of the Soviet Union at that time, which he described as a capitulation. I quite disagree with him. As he may not have been here when P. N. Fedoseyev spoke precisely to this point, I would like to emphasize his argument. Fedoseyev said, much better than I can say it now, that the problem for the Soviet Union at the time of the Cuban missile crisis was not to fight a war with the United States, but to prevent a war; but—and this is important—at the same time to guarantee that socialism would remain in power in Cuba.

That was the aim of the Soviet Union at that time. Now I ask Fann: What has happened? We all know what has happened. The war was prevented, and at the same time, socialism remained in power in Cuba. So, who capitulated, American imperialism or the Soviet Union? It is quite clear that the Soviet Union, through its chosen and well-thought-out policy, achieved the aims of progressive mankind and decisively defeated American imperialism. In my opinion, this is very characteristic of the policy of the Soviet Union, and I want to say this to Fann: socialism is not achieved and peace is not achieved by revolutionary phrases, but by a well-thought-out, well-reasoned foreign policy. So Fann will pardon me if I disagree with him on this point. On many other points, I quite agree with him.

What has impressed me at this colloquium is that we were able to discuss our differences in a constructive and creative manner. One should not be frightened that we as Marxists have differences on many important points. It only shows that Marxist philosophy is not static but dynamic, that it is not a dogma but a truth-discovering process—and this is what I found so impressive here. We have learned to create an atmosphere in which we can discuss our differences in a constructive and creative manner, helping each other to learn how to fight against imperialism even more scientifically and better than we have done in the past.

NOTES

1. Karl Marx, *Capital: A Critique of Political Economy*, Chap. 32, "Historical Tendency of Capitalist Accumulation." (New York: Modern Library, 1906), pp. 836-37.

12
Discussion and Replies 2

RONALD HIRSCHBEIN (USA)

On Wednesday, John Somerville began our colloquium by asking—and I'm going to paraphrase his question—what can be done to prevent our planet from becoming a dead cinder? But Somerville was no Cassandra in asking this question. In horrifying detail, he went into a little-known book by Robert Kennedy that chronicled the chain of events during the Cuban missile crisis of ten years ago, events that almost led to the nuclear annihilation of the entire planet. And the Kennedy brothers, despite their liberal veneer, considered annihilating the entire planet by hydrogen bombs an acceptable option.

This question so powerfully raised by Somerville raised in turn several related questions. Some of these questions have, I believe, been answered in our colloquium. However, what is perhaps the most crucial question remains an enigma. I think it is our obligation, as Marxists and humanists, to deal with this enigma. First, let us look at some of the questions that I think were rather plainly answered both by Somerville and by some of the other speakers. For example, what should our moral position be regarding the use of nuclear weapons? As humanists, it would seem insane of us to advocate a position that could very well entail the destruction of the human race. Surely, it is one of the basic assumptions of humanism that as the precondition of everything else human beings must exist. Hence, in regard to our moral position, I find myself concurring with Somerville that we must adamantly oppose the use of nuclear weapons for any reason.

The second question was: What should our theoretical position be regarding international conflict? I think that an examination of the Marxist tradition is very useful in helping us to formulate a theoretical position. Marx's monumental achievement was in being able to relate things that were previously unrelated, in being able to sensitize us to realities that had theretofore been obfuscated, at least in bourgeois consciousness. The theoretical position of Marxism, then, is that predatory capitalist nations promulgate warfare. Wars are actually in the interest of predatory nations. Marx, of course, went into great theoretical detail, which we don't have to rehearse here, to show how warfare, aggression, and less obvious forms and more subtle varieties of violence are an inherent feature of capitalist economic foreign relations. So these two questions—the question of morality and the question of theory—are pretty clear when it comes to warfare.

But judgments and theories are not enough, as one of the speakers in our colloquium eloquently pointed out when he referred to Marx's eleventh thesis on Feuerbach—that philosophers must not only understand the world; they also must change the world. And that brings us to the most vexing question of all, the most problematic issue, the question that unhappily is still, at least to my mind, an enigma in our colloquium: What must we do, what can we do to prevent the nuclear incineration that would leave no survivors?

This most crucial question could only be answered through predictive science. It's not enough to have a science that makes a strident moral judgment about nuclear warfare. It's not enough to have merely theoretical understanding. These conditions are necessary but not sufficient. We must have a predictive science. This brings us to the question: In its contemporary formulation, in its contemporary state of development, is Marxism a predictive science? Our answer, I think, must be that, in light of the evidence, it generally is not. Historically speaking, Marx did predict that revolutions would occur in the hundred years after he wrote, and revolutions did occur in just about every country—except where he predicted. So we have to be realistic enough, as Marxists, intellecutally honest enough, to acknowledge that at least some of Marx's significant predictions have not come true. I'm sure that any Marxist here present would have been very happy if it had been possible to give us some very facile formula to prevent nuclear incineration. But no such facile formula is available. Unlike Newton or Einstein, we cannot come up with a precise and accurate mathematical formula for preventing nuclear disaster.

This brings us, then, to the question that I would formulate as follows: Why is Marxism not a predictive science as yet? I do not want to denigrate any of the valid predictions Marx has made, although I would think it self-delusive to believe that Marxism has become a fully established predictive science with the status of a field like physics. I think that one of the reasons that Marxism as yet has failed to become a predictive science is what has often been called a cultural lag. We as Marxists use a metaphysics of science that is, after three or four hundred years, very outdated. What I mean specifically is that some Marxists seem to have a metaphysical position quite similar to that of bourgeois materialists and Anglo-American social scientists. Some Marxists seem to have interjected into their science an absolutistic Newtonian metaphysics that Lukács and other Marxists rightly criticize as bourgeois materialism, the universal reduction of everything to matter in motion.

This type of mechanical reductionism that reduces human consciousness itself to a machine has pernicious consequences for consciousness. But more importantly for our consideration right now, this type of outdated Newtonian reductionism has inadequate predictive powers for the external world, that is, for the social relationships in the external world. But what can be done if the Newtonian paradigm is inadequate for Marxism? Has there been any progress in science since Newton and the crude notion that everything is some sort of mechanical matter in motion?

Happily, the answer is yes. We can overcome this cultural lag and adopt a much more humanistic metaphysics, one which is much more closely attuned to Marxist ideas of ongoing dialectics and to ideas associated with the term *aufgehoben*. That is, we can adopt the metaphysics of Heisenberg and Einstein, a metaphysics that affirms that man is not a machine, but is an active agent intervening in the knowing process. He is an autonomous participant in the process of understanding and changing the world, not simply some sort of passive machine in the spirit of Newton. And in addition to that, if our Marxism is to be flexible, we can attempt to integrate the insights of the phenomenological sociologists. Their insights stress the role of intentional activity, of human autonomy and praxis in shaping the world. In my view, the problem that all too many Marxists fail to see is, to paraphrase Marx, that the dead hand of Newton rests on contemporary Marxism like a nightmare.

HOWARD L. PARSONS (USA)

I would like to make some remarks about the relation of ecology to the questions of war and peace, beginning with a response to Erwin Herlitzius. If I understand him correctly, he maintains that the problem of creating a planetary environment ecologically worthy of man must not overlook the class struggle, must not overlook the pollution of the worker in his place of work, and in his struggle against the dehumanization of the conditions of his life, the life of his family, the life of his class under an exploitive social system.

In one or another degree, I think these two positions are mutually necessary and reenforcing. That is, the worker must understand and we as intellectual workers must come to understand that the pollution we experience has its sources in the relations of production. But we also must come to understand that merely to correct those local or national conditions of ecological corruption, while it is necessary, is not sufficient. We must understand that we live in a single world, that the laws of ecology apply not only to one factory, to one farm, to one nation, to one continent, but to the whole planetary environment.

The context in which I think we must understand this question is a planetary context. Marx understood this. We have before us today two ecosystems—a capitalist ecosystem and a socialist ecosystem. They are in mutual struggle, and they are dialectically related. The two systems are antagonistic; they cannot survive together for long. This antagonism is evident in many ways. It has been evident for centuries, and the genius of Marx and Engels was to delineate this antagonism—its origins, its conditions, and, of course, its future.

Our Vietnamese colleagues here today have stated with striking vividness and moving humanism the extent to which the antagonism can go in a war that comes up to the threshold of nuclear destruction. In Vietnam, we can see the intimate relationship between technology and ecology. But my own government is, of course, the leader in this kind of antagonism toward a new social system. I will not recite all the figures with which we are familiar, which describe the brutal destruction of the Vietnamese people and the Vietnamese land—millions of people killed, injured, maimed, displaced; the land desecrated; the wild life destroyed; 26 million craters produced in Indochina over a period of more than a decade.

This is the result of the antagonism of a capitalist ecosystem in conflict with a new, rising, growing socialist ecosystem on the planet. And it must never be forgotten that the capitalist ecosystem is capable of destroying all ecosystems, including itself— the point that was made with devastating clarity by John Somerville. At the same time, these two ecosystems are united in the comprehensive, underlying, and overall ecosystem of the planet, so that they exist in dialectical interrelationship and must be understood as such. It would be a mistake to emphasize merely the antagonism at the cost of violating the laws of nature; a number of observations may be found in the works of Marx and Engels on this point. However—and I think this was Herlitzius' point—it would equally be a mistake to talk in a merely idealistic way, as many liberals do, about the ecological unity of the planet, forgetting the class struggle and the relations of production.

So I believe that the crisis in weaponry and the ecological crisis, which are really different aspects of the same crisis today, underline the same thing—first, the danger of escalating the antagonism to the point of destroying our species and, second, the necessity of overcoming this worldwide antagonism between two ecosystems. Now I maintain that, if what I have said is true, the problem of overcoming the antagonism in weapons is intimately related to, and inseparable from, the problem of overcoming the ecological antagonism between these two systems. That is to say, the relations of production and the class struggle must no longer be conceived in nineteenth-century terms, but must today be understood on a planetary basis, in terms of what we know about ecology.

This does not mean that the observations of Marx and Engels concerning exploitation, concerning the relations of production and the class struggle are false. Nor does it mean that they said nothing about ecology; they said a great deal. It means rather that, beginning with the relations of production, we must see that in the last hundred years these relations have developed to the point of imminent ecological and genocidal destruction, through processes that, although slower and less obvious than some others, do produce death. For example, it is a fact that all of us living today will live less long because of the pollution of the atmosphere by atomic testing. All of us taken together today represent the first set of people on earth who have a very large amount of strontium 90 in their bones. And so on. This is a new situation, qualitatively new, and requires, as Somerville underlined, a new theory and a new practice.

Thus, the problem of weapons cannot be understood apart from the problems of ecology. If we wanted to put it in general terms, the problem of weapons is an aspect of the struggle between two ecosystems, not only the class struggle within society, but the struggle to save the human environment, which is an organic part of humanity. One of the points of my thesis is that Marx and Engels were concentrating on the pollution of the bodies of workers in their places of work in the factories and in the rural slums, and at the same time, they made a number of comments about the pollution of nature. But the obvious fact to them in the nineteenth century was, of course, the direct suffering, the direct exploitation of the workers.

We have to put this in a new perspective, building on those insights. Therefore, I would say that it seems to me that the most important step, the most vital step, vital in the literal sense for us, is to preserve our species, present and future, which means the prevention of genocidal wars, the control and elimination of genocidal and biocidal weapons. These weapons represent a contemporary extension of the technological powers of man. And at the same time, I would emphasize that the existence of human life and all forms of life is threatened by a slower and less dramatic form of genocide and biocide in the occurrence of ecological injury and destruction.

Let me cite some of the evidence for this. The technology of atomic fission and fusion has given us the power of absolute death over all living matter, as well as the power to inflict genetic and somatic injury from the testing of atomic weapons by national governments. I hope you share my concern with the fact that quite recently (prior to 1973) several major powers have exploded nuclear bombs, releasing great amounts of radiation into the environment. And I have not read of any protests from any major governments. Some of the smaller governments have protested.

It is an established fact that such testing reduces the length of life, undermines the quality of it, and has long-range effects extending over many thousands of years on the living matter of this planet. Other new technical advances—such as the control of genetic materials, organ transplants, devastating methods of warfare, automation, contraception, abortion, drugs for altering states of consciousness and states of society, prolongation of life regardless of its quality, monitoring and surveillance, concentration and control of information, mind-manipulating media—all these advances of technology have put into question the values of this extensive power. The technologies of modern industrial society have introduced new elements into the cycles of nature, accelerating these cycles with harmful consequences to man. Inorganic materials, such as metals, nuclear waste and concrete, used and produced in industrial processes, get into natural cycles and cause injury or death to living organisms. In addition, man's release of stored energy in fossil and nuclear fuels accelerates the cycles of nature.

The by-products of heat, carbon dioxide, water vapor, carbon monoxide, sulfur oxide, and hydrocarbons interact with natural cycles, one result of which is smog in many of the large cities of the planet. Man's technological agricultural production can cause soil erosion, dust pollution, waterlogging of roots, pollution of drinking water, destruction of marine life, injury and destruction of insect and plant life. Harmful insecticides, herbicides, detergents, radioactive substances, and other materials have gotten into food chains and have adversely affected living things in the web of life wherein they are sustained. In my own country, the United States, according to Professor Barry Commoner, there can be found 37,000 synthetic chemicals available for use in industry, of which number only 8,000 have been tested, even superficially, for their consequences on man and nature. In the United States, more than half a million chemicals are produced that are largely unexplored as to their effects on man's health.

In conclusion, let me emphasize that there are two kinds of death—the dramatic kind, as in the genocidal weapons that we have, and the other kind, which I have referred to as ecological death. This latter kind takes the form of a shortening of life and an impairment of its quality. That is, while we live, we may be living under conditions in which much of the environment is being destroyed, injured, or polluted. And this kind of ecological death is increasing at an alarming rate. In this regard, our theoretical task is to affirm the truth of Marxism-Leninism, that is, the truth of the dialectical relations of man to nature.

In this connection, I think Hirschbein has something important to contribute. His last expressed concern was that Marxism-Leninism is in a kind of theoretical crisis, which, he suggested, has roots that go back to Newton's work. But I believe that is a misunderstanding of Marxism. I think that in the United States one of our problems is to speak to young people, to workers, and to all people in a way that shows that Marxism-Leninism is not a cold, mechanical summation of positivistic approaches to life, as it is often misrepresented to be, but that it is concerned with the interdependence and unity of person with person and of man with nature. This means that Marxism-Leninism has a deep devotion to the forms and processes that sustain us, to the beauty, harmony, and other values of our lives within the context of a sustaining nature, that it conveys not only a sense of gratitude toward life, toward the material universe, but also a sense of responsibility toward it.

We need to reaffirm and reformulate our position in vivid ways, in true ways, in convincing ways, in ways that Loeser called for in his presentation yesterday. That is to say, we must communicate with the young people and the mass of workers in a way that will show them that Marxism-Leninism is the only philosophy that has addressed itself to these vital questions during the last century and that it is capable of responding successfully to the crisis in technology and ecology today. If we cannot do this, the workers and the young people of our time will turn to the diversions, the entertainment, the drugs, and the "cop outs" that capitalist enterprise has ready for them. This defines a theoretical task.

A simultaneous and essential practical task is that of creating a peaceful environment, of getting those nuclear weapons out of Southeast Asia, out of Okinawa, out of Japan, out of all the U.S. bases in the world, to create a world that is free of genocidal and biocidal weapons. This, I repeat, is a *simultaneous* practical task, along with that of the ecological care of our planet, which Engels calls our one and only. I have argued that this task must be undertaken by peoples and governments, and I referred to the agreements between the Soviet Union and the United States during the last few years, which make a small beginning on these tasks. All of them have to do with the environment, beginning with nuclear arms and coming down to the specific control of pollutants. But this task must be extended on a worldwide basis. It must begin with the workers in their places of work, joining with their brothers and sisters abroad in international solidarity and proletarian internationalism. If this task is not undertaken, we will lose our lives, our children, our future, our planet, our one and all.

JOHN SOMERVILLE (USA)

I wish to say a few words about some comments that were made in relation to my paper. First, about wars of national liberation: I did not mean to suggest that I was opposed to wars of national liberation that do not become nuclear wars. I have always defended the right of any nation to take up a war of national liberation. On the other hand, no matter what the cause of the war is—national liberation or anything else—and no matter how just the war is in the beginning, if the war should become a thermonuclear contest, it would mean the end of humanity and doubtless the end of all life on the planet Earth. This is not national liberation; it is universal destruction.

In other words, the problem that I was posing is not the problem of denying the concept of the just war. No Marxist can deny the concept of the just war. But the truth is, we are faced with a new situation about war when wars can be fought with thermonuclear weapons, because nobody has a right to end the world; nobody has a right to destroy all humanity. Therefore, there is no right to a *thermonuclear* war of national liberation. In fact, a thermonuclear war would make national liberation impossible because it would destroy the nation.

Thus, the problem that I posed relates only to the use of thermonuclear weapons. And you cannot solve that problem by talking about a just war or a war of national liberation. Let me repeat: you cannot solve the problem of thermonuclear weapons by talking about a just war or a war of national liberation. If you are going to solve the problem posed by thermonuclear weapons, you need new concepts and new political strategies. That is all I was trying to say, and I think it is in accordance with the basic principles of Marxism to recognize that, when there are qualitatively new situations at the technological base of society, they demand qualitatively new principles and attitudes in the superstructure of society, at the political and economic levels.

This also means that I would differ very much with speakers who said that the existence of thermonuclear weapons does not change the nature of war. I think this is contrary to plain historical fact because in the past we always have meant by the word "war" a contest of military force after which there were still human beings left and a living planet Earth left, after which people could go on with their lives and nations would not completely disappear. That is the meaning of war—a physical, military contest in which it is possible to have a winner and a loser. Now when you begin to fight wars with thermonuclear weapons, you have reached a point where there will be nothing left to win, and no one left to be a winner or a loser.

Let us think for a moment of boxing; in my country, boxing is a very popular sport. As you know, stuffed gloves are used. The boxers try to hit each other and try to defend themselves, and one may knock the other out. This is what is called boxing. Now suppose we began to manufacture new boxing gloves so that in each glove there was a hand grenade or a stick of dynamite, so that when one boxer hit the other, he was dead; in fact, they were both dead. Would you still call this boxing? You would need a new word for this. So also, when you fight with thermonuclear devices, you need a new word for it. We might use the new word, biocide, or better still, omnicide. War kills millions of people, but it doesn't kill everybody. On the other hand, thermonuclear conflict can kill everybody, and not only every person, but every animal and plant, down to the last living cell, and everything created by life.

If you still call this war, you are deceiving yourself. And if you still call this war, people will think you are talking about the old kind of thing we used to have, and therefore, they will think that the same old concepts and the same old attitudes, the same old morality and the same old politics will be good enough to deal with it. But you would be deceiving yourself and others. Thus, when you talk about a physical contest with thermonuclear devices, it is qualitatively different from what we have been used to calling war. It is not a bigger war or a more dangerous war. If you think it is simply that, you would be using the logic of someone who says: you can get a little disease or a big disease, and if you die, that is just a bigger disease, just a worse disase, a more dangerous disease. But there is a qualitative difference between death and a very dangerous disease. From any disease, however dangerous, you might possibly recover and live on. But you cannot recover from death. Just as there is a qualitative difference between the worst disease and death, there is the same kind of qualitative difference between the worst war fought with conventional weapons and a conflict fought with thermonuclear weapons on both sides. That is the import of what I was saying. I do not deny the concept of the just war so long as it does not develop into a thermonuclear conflict.

The war in Vietnam remained a just war, from the side of the Democratic Republic of Vietnam, because, by the proper strategy and tactics, it was prevented from becoming a thermonuclear conflict. Since the invention of atomic weapons, wars have been fought in Korea, in Vietnam, and in other places. These wars have remained inside the boundaries within which the thermonuclear weapons had little or no probability of being introduced. The concept of the just war and the war of national liberation functions in these situations in the traditional way.

But in addition to such situations, we now are dealing with confrontations between major powers. We are even dealing with threats of the use of military force between major socialist powers. Are we not? We are in the presence of situations in which one major socialist power and another major socialist power are in positions suggesting military confrontations. In a few years, other major powers of the socialist camp may have thermonuclear weapons. Will the old concepts of the just war, will the old concepts of morality and politics take care of this situation that is developing? One thing is clear. We cannot solve the problem of preventing the end of the world if we accept the option of what is called nuclear war. If this problem is to be solved, it will have to be through new principles, new concepts, new attitudes, new tactics that, for the most part, we have not yet worked out.

Let me emphasize again what I have stated previously. I do not deny the distinction between just and unjust wars. What I am concerned with is a part of the classical interpretation of this principle. For in classical Marxism, the principle of distinguishing between just and unjust wars also was associated with the proposition that everybody capable should be ready to fight in a just war. It is not enough, of course, from the standpoint of the classical principle of Marxism simply to say that there is a distinction between just and unjust wars, but to refrain from fighting the just war. The implication of the principle in classical Marxism is that when the war is just we should be ready to fight in it, ready to risk our lives in it, ready to take part in it on the field of battle. Otherwise, this principle would represent a separation of theory and practice.

In this connection, it is important to notice that the Soviet government, by its very actions, has already recognized that there is a qualitatively new situation about war; and actions speak louder than words. In the Cuban missile crisis, the cause of Cuba was a just cause, but the Soviet government chose not to fight the just war. Why? The reason was that the war would have become thermonuclear. Take again the example of the Korean war. Surely the Korean war was a just war. But the Soviet Union did not choose to fight in that war. Why? I think the answer is clear. If the Soviet Union had come into the Korean war, in which the American forces already possessed nuclear weapons, it would have become a nuclear war. Therefore, the Soviet Union chose to use other means than to fight directly, physically, with military weapons. It chose to give Korea economic aid, logistic aid in the form of materials and weapons, political and diplomatic aid, but not to take up arms and fight. Consider also the war in Vietnam. Surely that, too, was a just war. However, the Soviet Union decided not to fight on the field of battle, but to give other kinds of help to Vietnam. In other words, the Soviet government recognized that, although the war was just, it would not have been a just or a right decision to fight in that war because to fight in that war would have created a situation far more unjust than the existing one. It would have created the concrete possibility of the destruction of the entire human race, the whole human world. That is why the Soviet decision not to fight in that war was entirely right.

What I am saying is that we must build on this principle that the Soviet Union has demonstrated in repeated actions. We must utilize this wise, humane, and successful principle. We must build on it as philosophers, helping to create a new moral principle, a new attitude, and a new education in this very important area. It is not enough that the right thing was done in action. As philosophers, we must explain why it was right; as educators, we must teach the principle that made it right. And we must recognize that it is not the principle that accompanied the old classical distinction between just and unjust wars. It is a new principle, the principle that when a war, whether just or unjust, can become thermonuclear, it is not in the interest of justice to destroy the human world by fighting that war with thermonuclear weapons.

In other words, if one side in a military confrontation is mad enough, insane enough to use nuclear weapons, should the other side use nuclear weapons in return, even though this would lead to the ending of the human world? Could that result ever serve the cause of human justice? In order to preserve the human world, it is necessary only that one side should understand that it would never be in anyone's interest to destroy the human world. So far, the Soviet Union has been that one side. It refrained in Cuba, it refrained in Korea, and it refrained in Vietnam from entering into a war that would have become thermonuclear, even though it was a just war, because in becoming thermonuclear, the just war would have become unjust. This may sound paradoxical, but it is good dialectics and good common sense. We cannot escape the conclusion that, in all cases where thermonuclear weapons can be used by both sides, where the human world would be destroyed by such use, it is obvious that the only solution is for one of the sides to use other means, as the Soviet Union has done in actual practice, for which it deserves the thanks of the whole world and of the future.

Let me here reply to certain specific arguments that have been offered against my position. K. T. Fann in his last intervention said: "It is true that the nature of world war is changing because of the tremendous destructiveness of nuclear weapons. But it also is true that, because the capitalists no longer possess a monopoly of nuclear arms, a new world war has so far been prevented." I believe this represents a complete ignoring of the plain facts of history that were clearly shown in the Cuban missile crisis. The documented facts that I cited about that crisis show, beyond any possibility of doubt, that a world nuclear war was not prevented by the fact that the capitalists no longer possess a monopoly of nuclear weapons. The documented facts I cited show, on the contrary, that even though the capitalist leaders no longer possessed a monopoly of nuclear weapons, they deliberately decided to send to the Soviet Union an ultimatum that they consciously expected would result in world nuclear war and the "end of mankind"—their own words, as cited from Robert Kennedy himself. What the documented facts further show just as clearly is that world nuclear war was prevented by the Soviet decision to withdraw its missiles unilaterally from Cuba (even though the American government refused to withdraw *its* missiles from Turkey).

Having closed his eyes to these facts, Fann says further: "If they [the capitalist leaders] are insane enough to unleash the nuclear weapons, then there is nothing we can do; there is simply nothing we can do." As he chose not to see that the capitalist leaders, by their own admission, showed themselves "insane enough to unleash the nuclear weapons," so also he chooses not to see that the Soviet action showed the kind of thing that can and should be done in such an event.

One last point: Professor Casteneda raised an important question about the participation of other philosophers—specifically Chinese philosophers—in our colloquium. I wish to assure him that I personally, as president of this colloquium and of the society that prepared it, wrote to the Institute of Philosophy of the People's Republic of China in Peking. I sent to them, beginning more than a year ago, at least three letters of invitation to participate in this colloquium, one in Chinese translation done by Professor Fann, but we did not receive an answer of any kind. There may be some good reason for this, possibly arising from the fact that they are still not prepared in their internal philosophical work to present their positions, and perhaps they soon will be prepared. In any event, this is of course a world congress; it is open to philosophers of the whole world, whatever their beliefs may be. We sought to invite philosophers of varying beliefs as a matter of principle, and had no desire to exclude anyone from participation.

Since this is our last session, I would like to thank equally all of those who have agreed and all of those who have disagreed with any one position. We are philosophers, and in relation to our disagreements, no better advice could be given than what Professor Loeser said here a short while ago, to the effect that we must learn to talk to one another, whatever our agreements or disagreements may be, in a constructive and helpful way. All those who disagreed with me have helped me, and I can only hope that I have helped those with whom I disagreed. Let us by all means look forward to further discussion.

Index

Aggression, Adolf Eichmann syndrome of, 97-98
Aldridge, Robert C., statement on American first-strike strategy, xi
Allende Gossens, Salvador, President of Chile: reasons for overthrow of, 122-23; significance of in relation to nature of imperialism as war, 93-95
American government, plutocratic control of, 57-58
American military bases, 60-61
Analytic philosophy criticized, 105
Arms race: and omnicide, 33; in relation to parity of weapons, 112
Automation, as part of contemporary technology, in relation to Marxism, 86-87

Baran, Paul, and Sweezy, Paul, their *Monopoly Capitalism* quoted, 61, 62, 63
Bebel, August, significance of policy of, in relation to Franco-Prussian War, 78-79
Bernal, John, quoted on profit incentive to arms production under capitalism, 62
Blackett, P. M. S., cited on conditions of massive use of nuclear weapons, 60
Burtt, Edwin A., his *Metaphysical Foundations of Natural Science* quoted, 99-100

Capitalism: and economics of war production, 60-63; and global nuclear war, 56-59; as source of wars, 3-4
Carter, President Jimmy: address at NATO meeting for increase of armaments, 46; failure of to address U.N. Special Session on disarmament, 46; statement of his willingness to make first use of nuclear weapons, x; the rejection by his administration of the thrice-made Soviet proposals for a mutual treaty of no-first-use of nuclear weapons, x

Index

China, People's Republic of: change of nuclear weapons policy in mid-1960s, 47; officially invited to the International Debate, 155

Chomsky, Noam, significance of his *The New Mandarins*, 58

Class, Marxist concept of, and war, 68-69

Class struggle, as motive force of history, 92-93

Clausewitz, Karl von, on war as continuation of politics, 92-93

Cold war: economic effects of in relation to capitalist production, 63; Soviet struggle against, 22; and testing of nuclear weapons, 59

Communist program best implemented under conditions of peace, 124

Computer science as part of contemporary technology in relation to Marxism, 86-87

Cuban missile crisis, 7-12; American government's expectation of world nuclear war and annihilation of mankind as consequences of its ultimatum in, 10-11; American government's ultimatum in, ix-x; central facts of, 8-12; criminality of American government's decision in, 55-56; Robert Kennedy's book on, 7-8; lesson of, as seen by American administrations from Kennedy's to the present, x-xi; lesson of, seen as Khrushchev's mistake, 136; and position of classical Marxism, 75-77; as refutation of theory of mutual deterrence, ix-x; in relation to human extinction, 33-34; Soviet view of, 18-19

Cybernetics, as part of contemporary technology, in relation to Marxism, 86-87

Defense spending, and capitalist economy, 60-63

Détente (relaxation of tensions), Soviet view of reasons for, 23-25

Deterrence, mutual, U.S. government's rejection of, xi

Disarmament, nuclear, as contrasted to arms coordination and arms control, 39-40; problems of inspection, control, and disposal of radioactive materials involved in, 43-45; U.N. Special Session on (1978), 34-38. *See also* Weapons, nuclear

Ecology, planetary: and class struggle, 144; in relation to capitalist and socialist ecosystems, 145-49; in relation to Marxism, 133-34, 144-49; relation to nuclear weapons testing, 147-49; relation to weapons crisis, 145-46

Eichmann, Adolf, syndrome: defined, 97-98; socioeconomic roots and conditions of, 131-33

Einstein, Albert, on possibility of nuclear ending of the human race, 33

Engels, Friedrich, on war and withering away of the state, 4

XVth World Congress of Philosophy, vii
Foreign policy, three basic options for U.S. in, 113-14

Ideology, analysis of in relation to peaceful coexistence, 129
Imperialism: nature of, in terms of aggression, intervention, conventional war, and atomic blackmail, 93-95; as source of war strategy of the U.S., 71-72; Soviet view of ideology and strategy of, 24
International Non-Governmental Organizations (NGOs), 34

Jungk, Robert, quoted on lethal effects of nuclear weapons testing, 60
Just and unjust wars: contrasted to good and bad wars, in Soviet view, 121; criteria of classical Marxism on, 78-79; and destructiveness of weapons used, 4-5, 25-27; Marxist-Leninist criteria of, 123; Marxist theory of, in relation to Franco-Prussian War, 78-79; need to modify position of classical Marxism on, 6-7, 25-28, 30-31; no need to modify position of classical Marxism on, 75-77, 134-35; position of classical Marxism on, 3-5; in relation to cold war, 77-78

Kant, Immanuel: Friedrich Engels's comment on, 98-99; his negative influence on modern consciousness, 98-105; Paul Lafargue's criticism of, 102
Kautsky, Karl, quoted on war and peace, 67-68
Kennedy, Robert: and Cuban missile crisis, 55, 56; significance of his *Thirteen Days* in relation to problem of human decisions to end the world, 7-8, 11-12
Khrushchev, Nikita, on nuclear war, 70-71

Leahy, Senator Patrick, statement of on overkill nuclear weapons in American and Soviet arsenals, viii
Lenin, V. I.: on class character of war, 68-70; on World War I, 79
Liebknecht, Wilhelm, significance of his policy in relation to Franco-Prussian War, 78-79

Marcuse, Herbert, quoted on sources of aggression, 103
Marx, Karl: significance of *Contribution to the Critique of Political Economy*, 12-13, 79-81; significance of his *Grundrisse* in relation to automation and problems posed by contemporary technology, 87-88
Marx and Engels: their *Communist Manifesto* quoted, 104; Engels's statement on their laying more stress on the economic factor than is due it, 104
Marxism: and contemporary problem of the pollution of leisure time, 87-89; and predictive science, in relation to

Newtonian reductionism, Heisenberg, and Einstein, 142-44; proposed solution in the spirit of Marxism and its relation to the prevention of nuclear war, 89-90

Marxism, classical: its position on the use and justification of war, 3-5; preconditions for entering into revolutionary civil war, 14; its relation to problem of preventing nuclear annihilation of mankind, 12-14, 48-49; relations of base and superstructure in, as applied to preventing nuclear war, 14

Marxism, contemporary: and need for new theory to deal with problem of nuclear war, 12-14; and technology, 85-86

Marxist-Leninist compromises, in relation to preventing war, 76

Marxist revisionism, and war, 68-72

Marx's concept of the universal person, 88-90; and real life as beginning with leisure, 87-89

May, Rollo, quoted on sources of aggression, 101

National liberation movements, in relation to economic interests, 116

Nixon, President Richard, significance of his blockade of Haiphong harbor, x, 27

Non-Governmental Organizations (NGOs): International, sponsorship of International Symposium on the Damage and After-Effects of the Atomic Bombing of Hiroshima and Nagasaki (1977), 34; nuclear policy of Japanese, 52-53; and policy on abolition of nuclear weapons, 42, 47

Nuclear blackmail: and American policy, x, xi; Soviet view of, in Cuban missile crisis, 19

Nuclear Non-Proliferation Treaty, 39

Omnicide, definition of, 151

Partial Nuclear Test Ban Treaty, 39

Peace: as needed by peoples and economies, in Soviet view, 24-25; as related to international law, in Soviet view, 22; world, as a weapon, 60-61

Peaceful coexistence: and blurring of class consciousness, 117; as common ground between capitalist and socialist countries for avoidance of nuclear war, 93; impeded by false ideologies, 130; Lenin's 1917 message and Soviet policy of, 75; and military-industrial complex, 129; and social progress, 28

Peaceful transition to socialism, concept of in relation to Allende's Chile, 138

People's Republic of China: change of nuclear weapons policy in mid-1960s, 47; officially invited to the International Debate, 155

Philosophers, responsibility of in relation to possibility of om-

nicidal nuclear conflict, 64-65
Philosophy, analytic, criticized, 105
Proletarian internationalism, and war, 78

Revisionism, Marxist, and war, 68-72
Revolution, in science and technology, 5-6, 63-64
Revolutionary civil war, Marxist preconditions for entering into, 14
Russell, Bertrand, on possibility of nuclear ending of human race, 33
Russell, Senator Richard B., quoted on excessive military spending, 63

SALT (Strategic Arms Limitation Treaty), 39
Schlesinger, James: his 1975 policy statement on American first-use of nuclear weapons, x
Science and technology, revolution in, as it relates to capitalism and socialism, 5-6, 63-64
Second International of Socialist Parties, in relation to war and peace, 67-69
Social-imperialism, danger of, 117
Socialism, Marxist, and nuclear weapons policy, 48-50
Socialist economy, in relation to need for peace, xi-xii, 61
Sorensen, Theodore: on Robert Kennedy's reflection concerning ethical question of government's right to decide about nuclear destruction of mankind, 11; as presumptive editor of Robert Kennedy's *Thirteen Days*, 11
Soviet losses of life in World War II, 127
Soviet nuclear policy, history of, 50-52
Soviet position: on humanism, 131; on nuclear war, 127; on war, distinguished from that of general pacifism, 122

Technology: and contemporary Marxism, 85-86; and improvement of prospects for peace, 109-10; in relation to national liberation movements, 115; and science, revolution in, 5-6, 63-64

United Nations 1978 Special Session on Disarmament, 34-38; analysis of Final Document of, 34-38; Japanese participation in, 34; mobilization for survival movement participation in, 34
United States government, plutocratic control of, 57-58
United States military bases, 60-61

Violence, role of in history, 94-95; Marxist view on, 94-95; sources of, 101

War: class character of, 68-69; concept of as continuation of politics and confusion in its interpretation, 92-95, 123-24;

economic incentives and disincentives to, under capitalist and communist systems, xi-xii, 61-63; global nuclear, no defense in, 56; and human rights, 4-5; imperialist, 68-69; main cause of, in Marxist view, 3-4, 6, 130; military-industrial complex as cause of contemporary, 22-23; moral evaluation of, by Marxists, 3-4; of national liberation, 68-69, 71-73, 150-52; position of Soviet Marxism on, 19-22, 25-32; problem of presidential, 15; revolutionary civil, Marxist preconditions for entering into, 14; between socialist countries, 138-39, 152

Wars, just and unjust: contrasted to good and bad wars, in Soviet view, 121; criteria of classical Marxism on, 78-79; and destructiveness of weapons used, 4-5, 25-27; Marxist-Leninist criteria of, 123; Marxist theory of, in relation to Franco-Prussian War, 78-79; need to modify position of classical Marxism on, 6-7, 25-28, 30-31; no need to modify position of classical Marxism on, 75-77, 134-35; position of classical Marxism on, 3-5; in relation to cold war, 77-78

War, nuclear: as basis of American foreign policy, x-xi; central facts that constitute the human problem of, vii; as debated by Marxists, vii; as leading to end of the human world, ix-x, xii, 6-8, 10-11; not prevented by knowledge of mutually assured destruction, 154-55; as qualitatively different from other wars, 150-52; Soviet actions in relation to preventing, 153-54; Soviet view of possible consequences of, 17-18; Soviet view of prevention of, 18-19, 32; wishful thinking about, viii-x

Weapons, nuclear: American first-strike, x-xi; American policy on first-use of, x; in U.S. and Soviet arsenals, 1975-1981, viii; morality of using, in reply to nuclear attack, 25-32; problem and differing policies of abolition of, 38-45; Soviet practice in relation to use of, 13-14, 27; Soviet proposal and American rejection of treaty of no-first-use of, x; Soviet view of first-use of, as crime against humanity, 21

Weiss, Peter, his *Marat/Sade* quoted, 97-100

About the Editor and Contributors

John Somerville. Born 1905. Ph.D., Litt.D. Professor Emeritus, City University of New York. Author, *The Philosophy of Peace, The Peace Revolution, The Crisis: True Story About How the World Almost Ended* (documentary play), *Philosophy and Ethics in the Nuclear Age*, and other books widely translated. Author-participant, international UNESCO projects on Human Rights, Interrelations of Cultures, and Inquiry into Freedom. Co-founder and American President, Union of American and Japanese Professionals Against Nuclear Omnicide; President, Special Colloquium of the XVth World Congress of Philosophy; President, Society for Philosophical Study of Marxism; Editor, translation quarterly *Soviet Studies in Philosophy*. Cutting Fellow, Columbia University; Rockefeller grantee, Stanford University; Visiting Lecturer, Japan, USSR, Bulgaria, Yugoslavia, Canada, and Czechoslovakia.

P. N. Fedoseyev. Born 1908. Doctor and Professor of Philosophy, Academician, Vice-president, USSR Academy of Sciences. Honorary Member, Hungarian Academy of Sciences; Foreign Member of the Academies of Sciences of Bulgaria, Czechoslovakia, German Democratic Republic, and Poland. Author of many well-known works in philosophy and sociology, including *Communism and Philosophy, Contemporary Dialectics,* and *Twentieth Century Marxism*. His work is recognized as having contributed greatly to the development of dialectical and historical materialism and to philosophical aspects of history and science. He has analysed the dialectics of modern social development, the interaction between productive forces and industrial relations, the role of masses and individuals in history, and humanism and the methodology of social sciences. The field of peace problems and international cooperation is one of his main concerns.

Shingo Shibata. Born 1930. Professor, Faculty of Integrated Sciences, Hiroshima University. Author, *Lessons of the Vietnam War: Philosophical Considerations of the Vietnam Revolution,* 1973; Editor, *Phoenix: Letters and Documents of Alice Herz,* 1976; *Alice Herz als Denkern und Friedenskämpferin,* 1977, all published by Grüner, Amsterdam, Holland; *Revolution in der Philosophie,* 1977, V.S.A., Hamburg, and more than twenty books in Japanese, dealing with a Marxist approach to human nature, individual personality, mental labor, the scientific-technological revolution, alienation, human rights, and democracy. Editor since 1977 of *Yearbook of Marxist Studies,* Tokyo, with contributions of foreign scholars translated into Japanese.

Debiprasad Chattopadhyaya. Born 1918. Litt.D. and first in class in Philosophy, Calcutta University. Professor of Philosophy since 1942, mainly in Calcutta, though occasionally also as Visiting Professor in different Indian universities. Main published works include *Lokayata* (also in Russian and Japanese translations); *Indian Philosophy* (also in German and Russian translations); *Indian Atheism* (also in Russian translation); *What Is Living and What Is Dead in Indian Philosophy*; and *Science and Society in Ancient India.* Member of the Academy of Sciences of the German Democratic Republic.

K. T. Fann. Born in Taiwan, 1937. Educated in the U.S.; taught philosophy at Cleveland State University, Florida State University, and is currently Professor of Philosophy and Chairperson of the department at Atkinson College, York University, in Canada. Editor-in-Chief, *Social Praxis,* an international and interdisciplinary journal of social sciences. Author, *Wittgenstein's Conception of Philosophy* and *Peirce's Theory of Abduction.* Editor, *Wittgenstein: The Man and His Philosophy; A Symposium on J. L. Austin*; Co-editor, *Readings in U.S. Imperialism*; and *From the Other Side of the River: A Self-portrait of China Today.*

Erwin Herlitzius. Ph.D., Humboldt University, Berlin; Ph.D. and Professor, Dresden Technical University. He is the author of several books and essays on philosophical problems of technology. An early activist in antifascist re-education, he graduated from the social sciences faculty of the University of Jena. Since 1964 he has taught courses on dialectical materialism and special problems concerning the impact of science on society. Chairman, GDR National Committee on the History and Philosophy of Science. In the 1970s he lectured at universities in many parts of the United States. At present his researches are concerned mainly with problems of socialist humanism and peace. For the title of the present book he would have preferred Marxism, Nuclear War, and the Striving for Peace.

Adam Schaff. Born 1913. Professor of Philosophy, Warsaw University. Member, Polish Academy of Sciences. Head, Institute of Philosophy and Sociology, 1957-1968. Member, Bulgarian Academy of Sciences, and Paris Academy of Political Sciences. President, European Coordination Center, Social Sciences, Vienna. Doctor, h.c., Sorbonne. Publications include *Conception and Word,* 1946; *Introduction to the Theory of Marxism,* 1947; *The Origin and Development of Marxist Philosophy,* 1949; *On the Question of the Marxist Theory of Truth,* 1951; *The Objective Character of the Laws of History,* 1955; *Introduction to Semantics,* 1960; *Philosophy of Man,* 1962; *Language and Cognition,* 1964; *Marxism and the Human Individual,* 1965; *History and Truth,* 1970; *Structuralism and Marxism,* 1975; and *Alienation as a Social Phenomenon,* 1977.

Adolfo Sánchez Vásquez. Born 1915. Doctor and Professor of Philosophy, National University of Mexico. Educated in Spain, studied at the Central University of Madrid. Member, Faculty of

Philosophy and Letters, National University of Mexico. President, Philosophical Association of Mexico. Member, International Institute of Philosophy, and International Committee of Esthetic Studies. Author, *The Esthetic Ideas of Marx; Philosophy of Praxis; Ethics; Rousseau in Mexico; Esthetics and Marxism; From Scientific Socialism to Utopian Socialism;* and *Science and Revolution: The Marxism of Althusser.* In English, *Art and Society* and *The Philosophy of Praxis.*

Ronald Hirschbein. Born 1943. Professor of Philosophy, California State University at Chico. Chairperson, Society for the Philosophical Study of Marxism, Pacific Division. Member of the Advisory Council, American Section, Union of American and Japanese Professionals Against Nuclear Omnicide. He is active in the American antiwar movement and the international struggle for nuclear disarmament. He has published articles on creativity and on admittedly unorthodox Marxist approaches to contemporary problems. He is currently developing a Freudian-Marxist critique of contemporary "Pop-psychology."

George H. Hampsch. Born 1927. Professor, Chairperson, Department of Philosophy, College of the Holy Cross, Worcester, Massachusetts. Author, *The Theory of Communism*, and numerous articles on Marxist philosophy and international relations. Lectured on problems of détente at the USSR Academy of Sciences Institute for the Study of the U.S. and Canada. Took part in a two-week Conference of American and Bulgarian philosophers on peaceful coexistence, and in the first meetings of American and PRC philosophers, which were held at Beijing University and Zhongshan University, China. Member and divisional Chairperson, Society for the Philosophical Study of Marxism; member, Advisory Council, American Section, Union of American and Japanese Professionals Against Nuclear Omnicide.

LIBRARY